CORPORATE FINANCE DECISIONS IN VOLATILE ECONOMIC TIMES

Giampiero Favato and Carole Print

iUniverse, Inc.
New York   Bloomington

CORPORATE FINANCE DECISIONS IN VOLATILE ECONOMIC
TIMES

iUniverse books may be ordered through booksellers or by contacting:

iUniverse
1663 Liberty Drive
Bloomington, IN 47403
www.iuniverse.com
1-800-Authors (1-800-288-4677)

ISBN: 978-0-595-52413-6 (pbk)
ISBN: 978-0-595-62467-6 (ebk)

Printed in the United States of America

Acknowledgments

The following peer reviewers provided helpful suggestions and comments on the papers collected in this book:

Roger W. Mills, Professor Emeritus, Henley Business School

Bill Weinstein, Professor Emeritus Henley Business School

David Ewers, Subject Area Leader, Henley Business School

The Editorial Team of the Social Science Research Network (technical review)

The Editorial Team of the Henley Centre for Value Improvement (HCVI) Discussion Paper Series.

Contents

Introduction

It is hard to pick up a newspaper nowadays without reading about credit crunch, weak economic outlook and imminent recession.

Troubled economic times are putting an extraordinary pressure on corporate managers, who have to make investment decisions under unprecedented uncertainty and risk.

Corporations have increasingly adopted prescribed textbook investment analysis. When times get rough, however, it is so much easier to put the blame on financial tools, rather than to review how managers use information and why they make the decisions that they do,

Consequently, financial derivatives might be blamed for the global liquidity crisis, while DCF could limit managers' ability to make innovative financial decisions.

The management of financial resources is based on methods which are often intuitive, sometimes more complex, yet always to be applied with common sense.

The aim of this book is to help managers to reflect upon the critical assumptions underlying the most relevant tools for valuation of corporate investments under uncertainty.

It offers a wide range of working papers, journal articles and case studies, which are the fruit of our recent experience in teaching, consulting and research.

This book is ideally suited to both managers and MBA students who seek to improve their critical ability to make value decisions based on an array of relevant investment valuation tools.

Chapter 1.
Investing in volatile economic times: Vulture Capitalism or Opportunistic Corporate Finance?

The animated analysts' debate generated by the stunning Microsoft's bid for Yahoo provides an excellent opportunity to review the fundamental principles of valuation and their implications on shareholders' value creation.

Senior executives and industry analysts share the same gloomy sentiment about the short-term future of leading corporations, shifting into recession mode and preparing to cut costs, freeze hiring and reduce capital spending as they brace for an economic slowdown.

Rising oil prices, sagging consumer confidence and the on-going credit crunch are prompting corporate leaders to put in place contingency plans to protect against the expected economic downturn.

Chief financial officers polled by Financial Executives International, an association of financial executives, and The City University of New York's Baruch College, reflected this negative mood about US economic prospects.

In the last quarter of 2007, CFOs' economic optimism touched its lowest level since June 2004, when the survey was first carried out, and recorded a 10 per cent fall over the previous three months.

Their concerns are likely to be reinforced by the International Monetary Fund, which recently slashed its forecast for US growth and warned that no country would be completely immune from what it termed a global slowdown (Guerrera and Allison, 2008).

Cash-rich financiers are preparing to pounce on US companies hit by the financial turmoil – moves that could herald a new era of "vulture investing".

After years pushed to the sidelines by high valuations and fierce competition from private equity, so-called "value" investors believe the financial and capital market crisis now offers a great opportunity to buy companies at bargain prices.

In a recent note to clients, the credit rating agency Standard & Poor's said that, as the number of ailing companies in sectors ranging from brokerage and banking to media and consumer products grows, "vultures begin to stir".

Analysts said that, aside from well-known investors, several hedge funds and private equity groups have been raising billions of dollars in anticipation of a sharp rise in the volume of distressed assets and companies (Guerrera, 2008).

The case for distressed investing today

"Distressed investing," also known as "vulture investing", is the ultimate expression of contrarian investing. It requires buying the stocks or bonds of companies that are in deep financial distress, often in bankruptcy, with the expectation that they will emerge from bankruptcy a new and improved and - debt-free - corporation. Distressed investors buy claims they believe will rise in value, and they may undertake a variety of legal and managerial actions to create this rise. These debts or claims typically trade well below 100 cents on a dollar of face value.

Distressed investors seek to profit from pricing inefficiencies. That is to say, they enter situations in which they believe the typically illiquid market for such claims has underestimated the improvement potential.

Such situations exist because the original claimants may have to sell quickly.

For example, they may be constrained to hold investment-grade debt only, or they may be financially unsophisticated – for example, trade claimants. To date, insufficient distressed buyers with true analytical, legal and operational skills have operated in the market to drive returns down to "ordinary" levels.

This strategy carries with it a high risk that a substantial portion of the investment may be lost if a company fails to turn around. However, because the debt is purchased at a deep discount, the downside risk is mitigated somewhat. Moreover, the investment also carries with it significant upside potential if the company's reorganization efforts succeed.

Speaking in general terms, distressed investors seek to profit from pricing inefficiencies and assess the following criteria before making an investment decision:

1. The reason(s) underlying the company's poor financial condition.
2. The restructuring options available to the company.
3. The debt's position within the capital structure.
4. The type of bankruptcy proceeding it has undertaken or is contemplating.
5. The investment's time horizon.
6. The likely exit strategy relative to the asset.

Distressed investment opportunities present themselves in cycles. Periods of opportunity for investors in distressed opportunities have often followed cycles of heavy below-investment grade debt issuance.

High-yield issuance in 2003-2005 appears to have equalled or exceeded the previous high of 1997-1999. New issuance in 1997-1999 hit a record of $500 billion, which was followed by record defaults peaking in 2002 at 15%, creating ample opportunities for distressed investors. Current default rates are below average, at 3-4% for high yield debt and 2-3% for loans. Defaults in 2003 were close to 4%; in 2004 and in the first half of 2005, defaults were below 2% (Distressed Investment Report, 2007).

Nearly every US Company has suffered from indirect exposure to the housing crisis. Until recently, however, write-downs of direct investments in land or mortgage-backed securities have been confined to the financial and homebuilding sectors. In the last quarter of 2007, a drug-maker, Bristol-Myers Squibb (BMS), announced a $275m write-off of the company's holdings of securities that were backed, in part, by sub-prime mortgages. The market value of a pool of securities owned by BMS has dropped from $811m to $419m, even though they were rated triple-A when purchased (Harrison and Bass, 2008).

Corporations are making the first move:

the Microsoft bid to acquire Yahoo

While private investors and hedge funds get ready to capitalise on corporate misery, optimism has grown since major company deals eased concerns that the credit crisis might be hurting corporate and economic activity.

In particular, the bold Microsoft move to acquire Yahoo signalled an emerging force in the market for corporate control: cash-rich companies could ride the credit uncertainty to make strategic acquisitions at bargain prices.

Microsoft Corp offered to buy Yahoo Inc for $44.6 billion, in a bold bid to transform two ailing Internet businesses into a worthy competitor for market leader Google Inc. In what would be the biggest Internet deal since the ill- fated Time Warner-AOL merger, Microsoft offered $31 per Yahoo's share, in cash and stock. The price was a 62 percent premium over Yahoo's same day close, but only about a quarter of what the Internet Company was worth at the height of the dotcom bubble in 2000.

Yahoo would give Microsoft dominance in Web banner ads used by corporate brand advertisers. It also attracts more than 500 million people monthly to sites devoted to news, finance and sports, and Yahoo Mail is the leading consumer e-mail service.

According to the Financial Times (5), critics say the two companies have too many overlapping businesses -- from instant messaging to email and advertising, as well as news, travel and finance sites -- and both are weak in the Web search market, where Google dominates. The article also reports that sceptics say Microsoft and Yahoo have very different corporate cultures and worry about a clash such as the one that marred AOL's $182 billion purchase of Time Warner in 2001, which is seen as the worst merger in recent history. Time Warner Inc is now valued at only $57 billion (Walters, 2008).

Yahoo valuation

Under the proposal, Yahoo shareholders could choose to get $31 cash, or 0.9509 of a share of Microsoft common stock. The deal in aggregate must consist of one-half cash and one-half Microsoft common stock, the software maker said. Microsoft's stock price at the time of the bid valued Yahoo at around $30, or a rich 57 times forecast 2009 earnings. In comparison, Google was trading at around 20 times forecast 2009 profit.

Together, Microsoft and Yahoo can offer a credible alternative for consumers, advertisers and publishers. In response to the offer, Yahoo, which few days earlier reported a 23 percent drop in fourth-quarter profit and announced it would layoff 1,000 employees, said its board "would evaluate this proposal carefully and promptly."

Investors applauded Microsoft's bid, sending shares of Yahoo up nearly 50 percent during the next-day trading. But the backdrop of the news was an Internet advertising market that had significant potential for growth but still faced some uncertainty. Google reported fourth-quarter earnings that failed to meet Wall Street expectations.

Some analysts said Microsoft was overpaying for a company that warned earlier that week it had faced "head winds" in 2008, forecasting revenue below Wall Street expectations. Global Equities Research analyst Trip Chowdhry said Yahoo was not worth more than $20 per share as its only worthwhile properties were Yahoo Mail, Yahoo Answers and Yahoo Finance (Ordoñez and Braiker, 2008).

Value Drivers of M&As

Was the Microsoft's bid too high or too low?

The animated analysts' debate generated by the stunning Microsoft's bid for Yahoo provides an excellent opportunity to review the fundamental principles of valuation and their implications on shareholders' value creation.

The price placed by the market upon a public limited company's shares is taken to be an indicator of its perceived success. The competition for shareholders as well as customers and the potential for hostile corporate raids that now span national barriers require that a company's share price performs well relative to the rest of the market and, in particular, within its own market sector.

The use of discounted cash flow analysis in financial strategy has been popularised as Shareholder Value Analysis (SVA), and follows the financial economic theory of the value of the firm which has been in existence for many years. In using SVA, the quest for management is to maximise the value generated from the business in terms of the projected cash flows that are discounted at the cost of capital.

By adopting this approach top management and the board of directors should be better equipped to answer the following basic questions:

Will the current strategy as conveyed within the corporate plan create value for its shareholders and, if so, how much?

How would alternative strategic plans affect shareholder value?

In principle, the approach can be applied throughout a company and be translated into a language for all levels of management and managerial functions. This means that alternative future courses of action may be compared and their desirability can be assessed by the process of discounting cash flows at the relevant cost of capital. The returns obtained from these alternatives can be converted into conventional accounting performance indicators, making the approach relevant and usable by all managerial levels. Of course, as we will demonstrate, the principles involved are not without their difficulties in terms of their application.

One major advantage of adopting a discounted cash flow valuation rather than an accounting approach is that life after the end of the current financial year is taken into consideration. In contrast to the accounting approach, where a loss in a particular activity this year may be regarded as unacceptable, discounted cash flow analysis takes a longer term perspective and recognises that it may well be desirable to accept such a loss in a year, if there will be a substantial profit in future years.

Those strategies that create positive net present values should, depending upon the quality of the assumptions made, increase shareholder value, whereas those with negative net present values are likely to reduce such value. The logic of the approach is straightforward but, as we will identify, there are some practical difficulties.

In order to apply the discounted free cash flow (DCF) approach to corporate valuation, a number of stages need to be followed:

- A projection is required of annual operating cash flows for the planning period in question for each business defined as being in the corporate portfolio.
- The cash flows, once estimated, must be discounted at the cost of capital relevant to the company during the planning period and summed to give the present value of projected cash flows
- The final stage, and often the most difficult in practice, is the estimation of the residual or terminal value of the individual businesses at the end of the planning period, discounted to its present value
- The total present value for any particular strategy is the sum of the present values of annual operating cash flows and the residual value. As indicated earlier, there are parallels between the net present value approach and the measurement of value derived from holding a share. Just as a shareholder will usually be concerned with dividend and capital growth potential, a company will be concerned with annual operating cash flows and the residual value.

Sources of value creation

The objective in undertaking strategic options like mergers and acquisitions is to add value. Of course, additional value may not result immediately and it may take time to capture. This is where an approach reliant on assessing future cash flows conveys distinct advantages over more traditional measures that focus on the shorter term. However, there will still be a major challenge to meet in ensuring that the additional value actually occurs!

How is value added from a merger or acquisition? Potential synergies may result, the benefits of which can be related to their impact on the seven value drivers of the Shareholder Value Analysis approach. For example:

1. Sales growth may improve because of being able to use the distribution channels of each organisation to sell the products of both.
2. Reductions in operating profit margins may be possible because of being able to use production facilities more efficiently.
3. Cash taxes may be saved by being able to plan the tax position of the new combined organisation. This area may be particularly beneficial for certain types of cross-border deals.
4. Fixed capital requirements may be lowered by being able to use available spare capacity for increased sales activity. There may also be an impact on replacement capital requirements, a good example of this being a decision to merge by two high street clearing banks. It may be possible to provide service to both sets of customers in the new organisation by cutting the number of branches.
5. Working capital requirements can be reduced if the two businesses have a profile of cash flows opposite in effect to one another. There may also be potential benefits arising from better debtor, creditor and stock management.
6. The planning period may be lengthened because, for example, the new larger venture increases barriers to entry.
7. The cost of capital may fall if access is obtained to cheaper sources of finance.

A second, and very important, source of value may also come from stripping out some activities/businesses. In this way the net costs associated with a merger or acquisition can be substantially reduced and the real benefits drastically improved.

What makes mergers and acquisitions particularly challenging is that obtaining good quality, robust financial information may be very difficult for an acquirer. On the other hand, for the organisation being acquired, a major difficulty may arise in understanding the basis for the value placed on the organisation by an outsider whose rationale might be based on a totally different view of its future potential (Mills, 2007).

Value is in the eyes of the beholder:

Microsoft-Yahoo potential synergies

The result of an acquisition can be measured as increased cash flows for the newly combined business, as compared to the sum of the cash flows of the two pre-acquisition firms. The value of a company can be shown to depend on the perspective taken. The same company in the hands of another owner may be able to create substantially more value

Furthermore, the DCF framework can be applied by valuing the acquired and target companies on a stand alone basis and then comparing the sum of the two values obtained with their estimated value as a combined entity, making due allowance for all potential synergistic benefits.

To be meaningful in managerial terms, such valuations require the identification of the key value drivers so that the potential sources of benefit can be understood and analysed.

Microsoft reported that the online advertising market was expected to reach nearly $80 billion by 2010 from over $40 billion in 2007. The software company forecasted at least $1 billion in annual cost savings for the merged entity, from synergies in areas such as combining engineering talent.

Bernstein Research said the Microsoft-Yahoo deal appeared to be less about expanded business potential and more about cost-savings that could be obtained shrinking redundant operations.

"We are relatively comfortable with (Microsoft's) estimate of $1 billion in annual synergies. It appears to us that the majority of the synergies are on the cost side," said the note from Bernstein analysts Charles Di Bona and Jeffrey Lindsay. "The Microsoft bid of $31 is very astute because it puts pressure on Yahoo's management to take actions that could unlock the underlying value of Yahoo! Assets, which could be worth upward of $39-$45 a share." (Auchard and Wu, 2008).

Giampiero Favato and Carole Print

References

Auchard E and Wu T (2008), Microsoft bids to buy Yahoo. Reuters UK, February 1, available online at: http://uk.reuters.com/article/topNews/idUK WNAS894220080201?feedType=RSS&feedName=topNews

Guerrera F (2008), 'Vultures' circle companies at bargain prices. FT.com January 31, available online at: http://www.ft.com/cms/s/0/26e7c1e8-d02f-11dc-9309-0000779fd2ac.html

Guerrera F and Allison K (2008), Mixed messages hold CFOs hostage to fortune. FT.com January 29, available online at: http://www.ft.com/cms/s/0/91822548-cea9-11dc-877a-000077b07658.html

Harrison C and Bass D (2008), Bristol-Myers, Ciena Losses Show Subprime Infection (Update2), Bloomberg.com February 1, available online at: http://www.bloomberg.com/apps/news?pid=20601109&sid=anvgqhQba cc4&refer=news

Mills R W (2007), Corporate Finance: a Managerial Perspective. Value Focus, first edition.

Ordoñez J and Braiker B (2008), Is Yahoo Worth $44.6 billion? Microsoft is paying a premium to catch up to Google. Newsweek, February 1, available online at: http://www.newsweek.com/id/107020

Turnaround Management Association (2007), Distressed Investment Report, March, Volume 1, Issue 1, March, available online at: http://www. turnaround.org/cmaextras/DistressedInvestingReport.pdf

Walters R (2008), Microsoft challenges Google's grip, FT Weekend, 2-3 February, page 8.

Chapter 2.
Selling England by the pound: NIKE scores with UMBRO takeover

This brief case study focuses on the valuation of the potential synergies leading to the share premium offered by Nike to acquire the control of UMBRO.

The deal

On 15/09/07 it was reported that UMBRO plc, the listed UK sportswear manufacturer, may become a takeover target. The speculation has been prompted following the announcement that listed retailer Sports Direct International plc has built up a 9 per cent stake in UMBRO, and the latter is a major supplier to Sports Direct.

On 03/10/07 it was reported that Sports Direct has increased its holding in UMBRO to 19,201,402 ordinary shares representing a 13.14 per cent stake. UMBRO closed at GBP 1.1075 on 01/10/07, the last trading day prior to the report.

On 18/10/07 it was reported that the board of UMBRO has received an approach which may or may not lead to an offer being made for the company. The identity of the potential bidder is not known. Currently, Mr. Mike Ashley, the Sports Direct tycoon, holds a 15 per cent stake in the company, but it has been suggested the bid may have come from another party. The shares in the company soared 25 per cent today and the company is now valued at around GBP 220 million.

Later on 18/10/07 it was reported that Nike may be the company behind the takeover approach for UMBRO. Both Nike and UMBRO have declined to comment.

On 23/10/07 it was announced that Nike Inc and UMBRO have come to an agreement on the terms of a recommended cash offer of GBP 1.95 per share to be made by NIKE Vapor Ltd, a wholly-owned subsidiary of Nike, for the entire issued and to be issued share capital of UMBRO by means of a court sanctioned scheme of arrangement. The offer of GBP 1.95 in cash per UMBRO share includes the shareholders entitlement to receive the declared interim dividend of GBP 0.0194.

UMBRO's existing issued share capital of 146,080,290 shares can be valued at GBP 284,856,565. The offer of GBP 1.95 represents a premium of 62.5 per cent over the closing price of GBP 1.20 on 14/09/07, the last trading day prior to the report that UMBRO may be a target. The offer represents a premium of 18.182 per cent over the closing price of GBP 1.65 on 22/10/07, the last trading day prior to the announcement of the offer.[1]

The rationale

The acquisition, Nike's first in three years, will increase its sales of soccer apparel by about 20 percent to $1.8 billion and help overtake Adidas AG in sales related to the sport by the 2010 World Cup, a goal the American shoemaker stated last year. UMBRO has 1,820 outlets worldwide and supplies shirts and shorts to six teams in England's Premier League. This is of particular importance in the United Kingdom, a top soccer market where Nike has struggled in past years. It also helps the company's business in emerging markets such as Russia, Latin America and parts of Eastern Europe, where soccer is the top sport.

UMBRO, though, has struggled to sustain growth after a World Cup-fuelled 2006 surge, with the wettest British summer on record hurting revenue at clothing retailers this year. The company said last month that 2008 profit will miss its forecasts.

"We are fully committed to helping UMBRO reach its full potential and we are delighted that UMBRO's board is unanimous in its support of our offer," said Nike president and chief executive Mark Parker.

Nike, which makes the football kit for the Brazil national team and English Premiership clubs Manchester United and Arsenal, is purchasing a group which also provides sportswear for the Norway, Republic of Ireland and Sweden football squads.

High profile players endorsing the UMBRO brand include England and Chelsea captain John Terry and his national team-mate Michael Owen.

"This is an excellent deal for all our stakeholders," UMBRO chief executive Steve Makin said of the Nike offer.

"It provides great value for shareholders and exciting prospects for our colleagues, partners and customers around the world."

Nike's offer is subject to approval by UMBRO shareholders and regulatory bodies. The US group's approach already has the backing of English football's governing body, the Football Association, which has worked with UMBRO for more than 20 years.

FA chief executive Brian Barwick said: "Nike has provided firm assurances that the FA relationship with UMBRO will be protected and enhanced, and we look forward to working closely with both companies moving forward."

Nike has expanded aggressively into the football market over the past few years and aims to become the world's leading football brand by the 2010 World Cup in South Africa.

Nike intends to operate UMBRO as a stand-alone affiliate brand in the same way as Converse, acquired in 2003.

The Nike-UMBRO deal is the last of a series of acquisitions in the sportswear sector. Earlier this year, German manufacturer Puma was bought by French luxury goods empire PPR (Gucci, Yves Saint Laurent, Boucheron, Balenciaga). In 2006, Puma's German rival Adidas took over US sportswear group Reebok.[2]

ANNEX 1: the Target

UMBRO currently manufactures all types of sports wear apparel including training gear and football boots. UMBRO products are manufactured in factories that are owned and operated by other companies. A rigorous code of conduct ensures that all UMBRO manufactures comply with strict standards of working conditions. All manufacturers are required to demonstrate compliance with the code before being authorised to manufacture UMBRO product for UMBRO and its international licensees. Compliance is then monitored on an on-going basis through announced and unannounced visits. In the event of a breach, UMBRO's policy is to work with the manufacturer to resolve the issue. However, UMBRO stands ready to terminate manufacturer contracts in the event of a serious breach and sustained non-compliance.

All UMBRO supplier factories are authorised by UMBRO centrally. Suppliers are required to sign a Manufacturer Authorisation Agreement ("MAA"), which sets out the terms of their appointment, including the code of conduct. UMBRO keeps a central database of factories listing details of latest visit records, agreed improvement plans and any breaches of the code. UMBRO and its licensees have dedicated expert resources that are responsible for implementing a programme of announced and unannounced visits to all suppliers to monitor compliance with the code of conduct and review progress. Together with our international licensees, UMBRO continually reviews how we monitor ethical compliance throughout our business and supply chain.

UMBRO has produced kits for many notable football teams since establishment; its first kit was produced in 1934, for Manchester City, which won the FA Cup that year.

Over the years UMBRO have also produced kits for major teams including Barnsley F.C., Flamengo, Lazio, Arsenal, Celtic FC, Club Bolivar, Cruz Azul, Botafogo, Manchester United, Tottenham Hotspur, Chelsea, C.A. Independiente, Linfield, Liverpool, Aston Villa, Leeds United, Finn Harps, Everton, Rangers, Deportivo La Coruña, Olympique Lyonnais, La U, Colo-Colo, Santos, Vasco, Atlético Nacional, Inter Milan, AFC Ajax, Universitario de Deportes, Liga Deportiva Universitaria, Celta Vigo, FC Twente, Málaga CF, CSKA Moscow, Hajduk Split, Dynamo Moscow, Torpedo Moscow, FC Moscow, West Bromwich Albion, Wolverhampton Wanderers, Nottingham Forest and Wisła Kraków. From the 2007/2008 season onwards, Siena,

Cagliari, Birmingham City, Blackburn Rovers, Hull City, Morecambe, Sunderland, Linfield, Lincoln City, West Ham United, C.D. Santa Clara, Rangers, Wigan Athletic and Heart of Midlothian will also be wearing UMBRO kits.

In addition to club teams, UMBRO also produced kits for international teams, including Iraq, Brazil, Scotland, England, Northern Ireland, Republic of Ireland, Chile, Colombia, Bolivia, Peru, Mexico, Norway, and Sweden.

However, UMBRO have suffered in recent years with many of the big clubs they provided for moving to the big two of Nike and Adidas (notably including Manchester United, Chelsea, and Celtic FC). In addition to this Puma have vastly increased their participation in football and now provide many national teams with kits. Still, UMBRO managed to retain their long-standing partnership with The FA and, often in cooperation with JJB Sports, gained contracts for a number of clubs in recent years, including Rangers FC and several English clubs.

UMBRO currently is the official sports manufacturer of the English FA Cup and official sponsor of the new Wembley Stadium. UMBRO will partner The FA in the further development of the National Football Centre (NFC) at Burton-upon-Trent, becoming the title sponsor of the Centre. UMBRO is also the exclusive supplier of footballs to The FA.

Players who have endorsed UMBRO include Michael Owen, Deco, Luis García, Barry Ferguson, Míchel Salgado, Rogério Ceni, Alan Shearer, Henrik Larsson, John Terry, David James, Richard Dunne, Yasuhito Endo, Tim Cahill, Dodô, Hernán Crespo, and Hugo Perez.[3]

ANNEX 2: UMBRO financials

PROFIT AND LOSS ACCOUNT

Consolidated data		31/12/2006 12 months thGBP IFRS	31/12/2005 12 months thGBP IFRS	31/12/2004 12 months thGBP Local GAAP	31/12/2003 12 months thGBP Local GAAP
OPRE	Operating revenue / turnover	154,786	154,525	140,375	127,392
TURN	Sales	n.a.	n.a.	n.a.	n.a.
COST	Costs of goods sold	95,924	94,330	96,195	90,959
GROS	Gross profit	58,862	60,195	44,180	36,433
OOPE	Other operating expenses	31,436	26,788	33,186	25,692
OPPL	Operating P/L	27,426	33,407	10,994	10,741
FIRE	Financial revenue	950	395	7,062	-1,453
FIEX	Financial expenses	1,762	2,405	2,647	4,510
FIPL	Financial P/L	-812	-2,010	4,415	-5,963
PLBT	P/L before tax	26,614	31,397	15,409	4,778
TAXA	Taxation	6,846	9,443	4,795	2,797
PLAT	P/L after tax	19,768	21,954	10,614	1,981
EXRE	Extr. and other revenue	n.a.	n.a.	n.a.	n.a.
EXEX	Extr. and other expenses	n.a.	n.a.	n.a.	n.a.
EXTR	Extr. and other P/L	0	0	0	0
PL	P/L for period	19,768	21,954	10,614	1,981
EXPT	Export turnover	28,037	25,477	22,666	18,196
MATE	Material costs	n.a.	n.a.	n.a.	n.a.
STAF	Costs of employees	13,792	13,197	10,754	9,306
DEPR	Depreciation	1,367	1,421	5,658	5,513
INTE	Interest paid	1,762	2,405	2,647	4,510
CF	Cash flow	21,135	23,375	16,272	7,494
AV	Added value	43,535	48,420	34,468	24,107
EBIT	EBIT	27,426	33,407	10,994	10,741
EBTA	EBITDA	28,793	34,828	16,652	16,254

BALANCE SHEET

Consolidated data		31/12/2006 12 months thGBP IFRS	31/12/2005 12 months thGBP IFRS	31/12/2004 12 months thGBP Local GAAP	31/12/2003 12 months thGBP Local GAAP
FIAS	Fixed assets	84,706	84,393	69,581	73,847
IFAS	Intangible fixed assets	77,879	78,401	65,841	70,431
TFAS	Tangible fixed assets	2,517	2,662	3,740	3,416
OFAS	Other fixed assets	4,310	3,330	0	0
CUAS	Current assets	45,250	68,028	41,668	43,866
STOK	Stocks	11,931	7,259	6,733	8,605
DEBT	Debtors	20,159	24,693	15,058	19,864
OCAS	Other current assets	13,160	36,076	19,877	15,397
CASH	Cash & cash equivalent	4,732	1,580	8,936	1,512
TOAS	Total assets	129,956	152,421	111,249	117,713
SHFD	Shareholders funds	81,966	73,263	51,667	40,219
CAPI	Capital	1,445	1,445	1,445	47,751
OSFD	Other shareholders funds	80,521	71,818	50,222	-7,532
NCLI	Non current liabilities	9,139	21,581	12,849	11,682
LTDB	Long term debt	27	6,411	8,245	282
ONCL	Other non-current liabilities	9,112	15,170	4,604	11,400
CULI	Current liabilities	38,851	57,577	46,733	65,812
LOAN	Loans	41	11,316	7,829	24,422
CRED	Creditors	13,183	12,478	7,429	9,629
OCLI	Other current liabilities	25,627	33,783	31,475	31,761
TSHF	Total shareh. funds & liab.	129,956	152,421	111,249	117,713
WKCA	Working capital	18,907	19,474	14,362	18,840
NCAS	Net current assets	6,399	10,451	-5,065	-21,946
EMPL	Number of employees	269	225	198	193

ANNEX 3: the Acquirer

Nike, Inc. is the world's leading supplier of athletic shoes, apparel and sports equipment. Nike markets its products under its own brand as well as Nike Golf, Nike Pro, Air Jordan, Team Starter, and subsidiaries including Bauer, Cole Haan, Hurley International, and Converse.

Nike sells a huge assortment of products, including shoes and apparel for sports activities like Hockey, basketball, combat sports, tennis, Football, American football, athletics, golf and cross training for men, women, and children. Nike also sells shoes for outdoor activities such as tennis, golf, skateboarding, soccer, baseball, football, bicycling, volleyball, wrestling, cheer leading, aquatic activities, auto racing and other athletic and recreational uses. Nike are well known in Hip hop culture as they supply urban fashion clothing. Nike recently teamed up with Apple Inc. to produce the Nike+ product which monitors a runner's performance via a radio device in the shoe which links to the iPod nano.

Nike sells its product to more than 20,000 retailers in the U.S. (including Nike's own outlets and "Niketown" stores) and in approximately 140 countries in the world. Nike sells its products in international markets through independent distributors, licensees and subsidiaries.

Nike has a number of celebrity athletes and professional teams to focus attention on their products. Nike has signed top athletes in many different sports such as professional football (soccer) players Cristiano Ronaldo, Wayne Rooney, Ronaldo, Robinho and Ronaldinho.

Because Nike creates goods for a wide range of sports, they have competition from every sports and sports fashion brand. After surpassing Adidas in the 1970s, Nike had no direct competitors because there was no single brand which could compete directly with Nike's range of sports and non-sports oriented gear until Reebok came along in the 1980s. Reebok now has merchandising contracts with the National Football League and the National Hockey League in the United States, and was purchased in 2006 by Adidas. Nike's other competitor is Puma, the third largest shoe and sports clothing supplier.

Nike has more than 500 locations around the world and offices located in 45 countries outside the United States. Most of the factories are located in

Asia, including China, Taiwan, India, Turkey, Thailand, Vietnam, Pakistan, Philippines, Malaysia, and Korea. Nike is hesitant to disclose information about the contract companies it works with. However, due to harsh criticism from some organizations like Barbie.com, Nike has disclosed information about its contract factories in its Corporate Governance Report. Nike plans to be carbon neutral by 2011. Nike has been criticized for contracting with factories in countries such as China, Vietnam, Indonesia and Mexico. Vietnam Labour Watch, an activist group, has documented that factories contracted by Nike have violated minimum wage and overtime laws in Vietnam as late as 1996, although Nike claims that this practice has been halted. The company has been subject to much critical coverage of the often poor working conditions and exploitation of cheap overseas labour employed in the free trade zones where their goods are typically manufactured. Sources of this criticism include Naomi Klein's book No Logo and Michael Moore's documentaries.[4]

ANNEX 4: NIKE financials

INCOME STATEMENT

	Cons 31/05/2007 12 months Unqual th USD 10-K US GAAP	Cons 31/05/2006 12 months Unqual th USD 10-K US GAAP	Cons 31/05/2005 12 months Unqual th USD 10-K US GAAP	Cons 31/05/2004 12 months Unqual th USD 10-K US GAAP
30205 Operating Revenue / Turnover	16,325,900	14,954,900	13,739,700	12,253,100
30210 Sales	16,325,900	14,954,900	13,739,700	12,253,100
30215 Costs of Goods Sold	-8,885,800	-8,076,100	-7,357,800	-6,734,200
30220 Gross Profit	7,440,100	6,878,800	6,381,900	5,518,900
30225 Other Operating Items	-5,027,800	-4,482,200	-4,250,800	-3,776,700
30230 Depreciation/Amortization	-279,600	-291,800	-266,500	-267,200
30235 Operating P/L	2,132,700	2,104,800	1,864,600	1,475,000
30245 Financial Expenses	n.a.	n.a.	n.a.	n.a.
30250 Financial P/L	67,200	36,800	-4,800	-25,000
30260 P/L before Tax	2,199,900	2,141,600	1,859,800	1,450,000
30265 Taxation	-708,400	-749,600	-648,200	-504,400
30270 P/L after Tax	1,491,500	1,392,000	1,211,600	945,600
30275 Extraord. & Oth. Items	n.a.	n.a.	n.a.	0
30280 P/L for Period	1,491,500	1,392,000	1,211,600	945,600
30295 Cash Flow	1,771,100	1,683,800	1,478,100	1,212,800
30310 EBIT	2,132,700	2,104,800	1,864,600	1,475,000
30320 EBITDA	2,412,300	2,396,600	2,131,100	1,742,200

BALANCE SHEET

	Cons 31/05/2007 12 months Unqual th USD 10-K US GAAP	Cons 31/05/2006 12 months Unqual th USD 10-K US GAAP	Cons 31/05/2005 12 months Unqual th USD 10-K US GAAP	Cons 31/05/2004 12 months Unqual th USD 10-K US GAAP
30005 Current Assets	8,076,500	7,346,000	6,351,100	5,528,600
30010 Stocks	2,121,900	2,076,700	1,811,100	1,650,200
30015 Debtors	2,494,700	2,382,900	2,262,100	2,120,200
30020 Others	3,459,900	2,886,400	2,277,900	1,758,200
30025 Cash & Cash Equivalent	2,847,000	2,303,000	1,824,700	1,228,800
30030 Fixed Assets	2,611,800	2,523,600	2,442,500	2,380,100
30035 Tangible Fixed Assets	1,678,300	1,657,700	1,605,800	1,611,800
30040 Intangible Fixed Assets	540,700	536,300	541,500	501,700
30045 Other Fixed Assets	392,800	329,600	295,200	266,600
30050 Total Assets	10,688,300	9,869,600	8,793,600	7,908,700
30055 Current Liabilities	2,584,000	2,612,400	1,999,200	2,030,500
30060 Loans	30,500	255,300	6,200	6,600
30065 Creditors	1,040,300	952,200	775,000	780,400
30070 Other	1,513,200	1,404,900	1,218,000	1,243,500
30075 Non Current Liabilities	1,078,600	971,700	1,149,900	1,096,200
30080 Long Term Debt	409,900	410,700	687,300	682,400
30085 Other Non Current Liabilities	668,700	561,000	462,600	413,800
30090 Shareholders Funds	7,025,700	6,285,500	5,644,500	4,782,000
30095 Capital	3,100	3,100	3,100	3,100
30100 Other	7,022,600	6,282,400	5,641,400	4,778,900
30105 Total Shareh. Funds & Liab.	10,688,300	9,869,600	8,793,600	7,908,700
30108 Enterprise Value	19,042,302	21,102,005	22,168,319	19,713,190
30110 Working Capital	3,576,300	3,507,400	3,298,200	2,990,000
30112 Net Current Assets	5,492,500	4,733,600	4,351,900	3,498,100
30115 Total Liabilities & Debt	3,662,600	3,584,100	3,149,100	3,126,700
30120 Number of Employees	30,200	28,000	26,000	24,667

Brief discussion of the case

Sportswear Companies have become attractive targets for M&A, regardless of the volatility of sales growth typical of this industry sector. Sport brands are rapidly moving from sportswear to fashion. A clear example is Puma: the rampant feline left the sport courts to find a less volatile position on teenagers' casual shoes and bags. This motivated the interest of Gucci in acquiring the brand. A successful transition from sportswear to teenage fashion would expand the consumers' target of the brand, increasing the value of the franchising by increasing revenues (larger number of potential buyers), reducing marketing costs (market share less dependent upon champions' endorsement) and maintaining a premium price (entry level of fashion/luxury market).

Nike intends to operate UMBRO as a stand-alone affiliate brand. The 195p offer for UMBRO is fundamentally based on the assumption to rapidly increase UMBRO's SGR to Nike level (9%), maintaining the current OPM (18% of sales). Becoming a fully integrated subsidiary, UMBRO's WACC is supposed to increase to the level of Nike Inc (8.2%).

Year		1	2	3	4	5	6	7	8	9	10	Beyond
		%	%	%	%	%	%	%	%	%	%	%
Sales Growth Rate (SGR)		7%	9%	9%	9%	9%	9%	9%	9%	9%	9%	0%
Operating Profit Margin (OPM% sales)		18.0%	18.0%	18.0%	18.0%	18.0%	18.0%	18.0%	18.0%	18.0%	18.0%	8.2%
Cash Tax Rate (CTR% of OPM)		35%	35%	35%	35%	35%	35%	35%	35%	35%	35%	3.5%
IFCI (% incr sales)		0%	0%	0%	0%	0%	0%	0%	0%	0%	0%	0%
IWCI (% incr sales)		0%	0%	0%	0%	0%	0%	0%	0%	0%	0%	0%
Cost of Capital		8.20%	8.20%	8.20%	8.20%	8.20%	8.20%	8.20%	8.20%	8.20%	8.20%	8.20%
Depreciation (% of sale)		1%	1%	1%	1%	1%	1%	1%	1%	1%	1%	1%
RFCI (= depr)		1%	1%	1%	1%	1%	1%	1%	1%	1%	1%	1%

Year	2006	1	2	3	4	5	6	7	8	9	10	Beyond
		£m	£m	£m	£m	£m	£m	£m	£m	£m	£m	£m
Sales Receipts	149.5	159.2	173.5	189.2	206.2	224.7	243.9	264.6	287.1	311.5	337.9	337.9
Operating Profit		28.7	31.2	34.0	37.1	40.5	43.9	47.6	51.7	56.1	60.8	27.8
Less: Cash Tax		10.0	10.9	11.9	13.0	14.2	15.4	16.7	18.1	19.6	21.3	9.7
Profit After Tax		18.6	20.3	22.1	24.1	26.3	28.5	31.0	33.6	36.4	39.5	18.1
Add: Depreciation		1.6	1.7	1.9	2.1	2.2	2.4	2.6	2.9	3.1	3.4	3.4
Operating Cash Flow		20.2	22.0	24.0	26.2	28.5	31.0	33.6	36.5	39.6	42.9	21.5
Less: RFCI		1.6	1.7	1.9	2.1	2.2	2.4	2.6	2.9	3.1	3.4	3.4
Less: IFCI		0.0	0.0	0.0	0.0	0.0	0.0	0.0	0.0	0.0	0.0	0.0
Less: IWCI		0.0	0.0	0.0	0.0	0.0	0.0	0.0	0.0	0.0	0.0	0.0
Free Cash Flow		18.6	20.3	22.1	24.1	26.3	28.5	31.0	33.6	36.4	39.5	18.1
Cumulative WACC		1.0820	1.171	1.267	1.371	1.483	1.605	1.736	1.879	2.033	2.199	
Present Value (Free Cash Flow)		17.2	17.3	17.5	17.6	17.7	17.8	17.8	17.9	17.9	18.0	
Cumulative Present Value		17.2	34.6	52.0	69.6	87.4	105.1	123.0	140.9	158.8	176.8	
Present Value of Terminal Value											100.2	
Value of operating assets of the Firm											277.0	
% Terminal Value											36.2	
Cumulative Present Value of Free Cash Flows											176.8	
+ Present Value of Terminal Value											100.2	
= Business Value											277.0	
+ Cash and Marketable Securities											4.6	
- Market Value of Debt											0.0	
- Value of Equity Options											0.0	
= Corporate Value											281.6	

Value per share (144.6 million shares outstanding)	£1.95
UMBRO actual share price 14/09/2007	£1.20

Beyond any economic or financial rationale supporting the acquisition, governance issues could still jeopardise the full realisation of the prospective value synergies:

1. Market dominance: the Nike-UMBRO combined market share of football sportswear could negatively impact the ability of individual players, clubs, national teams (FA), and international football associations (UEFA, FIFA) to maximize the value of endorsement contracts. Regulators could ultimately decide to take actions against the Nike-UMBRO's dominant position, reducing the Value of synergies between the two brands.

2. Corporate Social Responsibility (CSR): the different sensitivity to labor issues could lead to disruptive tensions within the organisation, facing the challenge to manage a two-tier supply chain.
   The conflict could lead to a deterioration of the relationship with the current UMBRO's pool of "CSR certified" suppliers, on the basis of cost issues. On the brighter side, UMBRO's best practices could accelerate the rate of change in Nike's supply chain management, apparently a top priority for the American sportswear giant.

Chapter 3.
New M&A strategies: the RBS case[5]

Will the RBS consortium's approach become a trend and thus open up potential corporate holdings that were previously thought out of reach?

This case looks at the advantages and drawbacks of group bidding, such as the problem of diversification for conglomerates and the market's tendency to value them at a discount to more focused companies.

The RBS consortium

What began as an agreement between ABN Amro and Barclays to merge the two banks' operations escalated into a Europe-wide bid battle. The Royal Bank of Scotland Group plc. (RBS) consortium, which also includes Banco Santander SA of Spain and the Belgian-Dutch bank Fortis NV, claimed victory in a seven-month battle, making a higher - largely cash - offer.

Although Barclays, which had originally made a €66bn all-share offer, softened its approach with cash, its bid still lagged behind the RBS-led proposal, which valued the Dutch bank at €72bn.

Barclays rose 2.3% in London before its bid for ABN was to have expired Thursday October 4, leaving only the RBS consortium in the race to acquire the Dutch bank. RBS rose 1.6% and Fortis gained 5.4%. Trading in ABN Amro was suspended.[6]

The ABN takeover could become either a symbol of the exuberance seen in the recent M&A boom or a precedent to deals of a size previously thought out of reach in corporate finance.

Group bidding is not a new tactic in corporate finance: consortiums have already been put together few times since the 80s, mostly in Europe. They are rarer in U.S. because tax laws make it too costly to break up target companies efficiently. In 1988, General Electric Co. of the UK, known as GEC, became a pioneer in the field when it teamed up with Siemens AG to purchase the British electrical equipment manufacturer Plessey Co for $3 billion. In 2004, the French drinks firm Pernod Ricard SA teamed up with the American Fortune Brands Inc. to acquire the British Allied Domecq Plc for $17.8 billion and divide its portfolio of brands between them. This year, the Dutch chemical company Akzo Nobel was able to raise its bid for the British rival Imperial Chemical Industries (ICI) Plc. By joining forces with the German Henkel KGaA, after earlier being rejected by ICI (Singer, 2007).

The RBS consortium's approach might become a trend, because it ignites the creativity of the investment bankers advising corporate clients. It has long been a dream of M&A strategists to pick apart conglomerates composed of diversified divisions, and the consortium bid allows acquirers to pay a higher price and allocating pieces of the target to buyers who most value those assets. As a result, an entire tier of corporate holdings previously thought out of reach could become potential targets.

Size on its own is no longer a safety net

Conglomerates are companies that either partially or fully own a number of other companies, which may be in the same or in different industries. Titan holdings, such as General Electric or Unilever, were built up over many years with interests ranging from avionics to premium ice cream.

The case for conglomerates can be summed up in one word: diversification. According to financial theory, because the business cycle affects industries in different ways, diversification results in a reduction of investment risk. A downturn suffered by one subsidiary, for instance, can be counterbalanced by stability, or even expansion, in another venture. In other words, if GE's credit division has a negative performance, the loss might be offset by a growth in its jet engines business. However, the prominent success of conglomerates such as General Electric is hardly proof that conglomeration is always a successful corporate strategy. Peter Lynch uses the phrase "diworsification" to describe companies that diversify into areas beyond their core competencies (Lynch and Rothchild, 1994).

A conglomerate can often be inefficient. No matter how experienced the management team, its energies and resources will be split over numerous businesses, which may or may not be synergistic. For investors and financial analysts, conglomerates can be particularly hard to understand, and it can be a challenge to collocate these companies into one category or investment theme. Furthermore, a conglomerate's accounting can leave a lot to be desired and can obscure the performance of the conglomerate's separate divisions.

Investors' inability to understand a conglomerate's philosophy, direction, goals and performance can eventually lead to share underperformance.

Conglomerates do not always offer investors an advantage in terms of diversification. If investors want to diversity risk, they can do so by themselves, by investing in a few "pure players" rather than investing in a single conglomerate. Investors can do this far more cheaply and efficiently than even the most acquisitive conglomerate can. The case against conglomerates is a strong one. Consequently, the market usually applies a discount to the sum-of-parts, value - that is, it frequently values conglomerates at a discount to more focused companies (Mansi and Reeb, 2002).

The calculation of the discount can be exemplified by using a fictional conglomerate called Pimlico plc, which consists of two unrelated businesses: a media division and a fine chemicals division.

Pimlico plc has a market capitalisation of £4 billion and total debt of £1.5 billion. Its media division has balance sheet assets of £2 billion, while its fine chemicals division has £1.5 billion worth of assets. Focused companies in the media industry have median market-to-book values of 2.5, while pure play fine chemical firms have market-to-book values of 2. Pimlico plc's divisions are fairly typical companies in their industries. From this information, we can calculate the conglomerate discount:

Total Market Value Pimlico plc:
= Equity + Debt
= £4 billion + £1.5 billion
= £5.5 billion

Estimated Value Sum of the Parts:
= Value of fine chemical division + Value of media division
= (£1.5 billion X 2) + (£2 billion X 2.5)
= £3 billion + £5 billion

= £8.0 billion
 The conglomerate discount amounts to:
 = (£8.0 billion - £5.5 billion)/£8 billion
 = 31.25%

It becomes clear that this multi-business company could be worth significantly more if it were broken up into individual businesses. Consequently, investors may push for divesting or spinning off its media and fine chemical divisions to create more value.

Activist investors have been increasingly pushing for companies to break themselves up. One hedge fund's letter to ABN Amro demanding it put itself up for sale in whole or in parts helped push it into play. Then Peter Paul de Vries, the feisty head of the Dutch shareholder association VEB, successfully took ABN Amro's management to court, accusing it of bypassing shareholders when selling one of the bank's most attractive assets.

The efforts seem to be persuading executives that they need to listen to shareholders or risk their jobs and control over their company.

Rijkman W. J. Groenink, ABN Amro's chief executive, in an emotional outburst on April 28, complained to a Dutch court that his company had become "a toy for hedge funds."

Senior executives are also being pressured to deliver shareholder returns as the investment base of companies' shifts from passive institutional investors with longer-term horizons to hedge funds focused on the short term. Even though shareholder activism is generally considered to be positive because it makes companies more efficient and increases shareholder returns, some analysts said that the focus on short-term returns can mean important long-term goals were neglected. The three buyers of ABN Amro will immediately be under pressure to prove the consortium did not overpay for the deal or stretch its resources too far in pursuing such a complex corporate break-up.

Consortium strategy does not help to value synergies

The consortium members will begin dividing ABN's assets. RBS will take control of ABN's corporate bank, which provides trade finance, cash management and debt sales. Santander gets ABN operations in Italy (Banca

Antonveneta) and Brazil (Banco Real). Fortis will take ABN's private bank, making Fortis Europe's third largest player in private banking, behind UBS AG and Credit Suisse Group.

RBS could have drawn the shortest straw. While the corporate bank provides a good strategic fit for RBS's existing business in bonds and cash management, the acquisition comes at a time when credit markets are in troubled waters, limiting the ability to generate incremental business by issuing bonds for corporations. More important, RBS is not getting LaSalle Bank in Chicago, one of the assets that attracted RBS to bid for ABN in the first place. RBS sold the idea of the consortium to its shareholders partly on the premise that LaSalle would complement its current U.S. operations in the Northeast and Midwest. ABN sold LaSalle to Bank of America Corp., a $21 billion surprise move that RBS was unable to reverse.

A potential pitfall for Santander is that it will have to avoid ABN's failure to integrate its vast holding. The deal could be transformational for Fortis, whose current core competences are related to savings and insurance.

According to Moody's commentary (2008), Fortis and Santander emerged as clear winners from the successful takeover of ABN Amro.

In affirming Fortis' ratings (Aa3 stable), Moody's noted the good strategic fit with ABN AMRO's businesses to be acquired as well as the expected reasonable impact of the funding package on the capital structure, capitalisation and underlying fundamentals of the group.

"With this deal, there is a clear potential for Fortis to significantly enhance its franchise in the Benelux region," said Jose Morago, a Moody's Assistant Vice-President/Analyst. "Our stable outlook is predicated on the expectation that Fortis will continue to deliver satisfactory operating results, maintain its risk profile and restore its capital position and financial flexibility in the coming months. However, there are material challenges in the short-to-medium term, given the size, complexity and amount of resource necessary for Fortis to integrate and extract value from the new ABN AMRO businesses," Mr Morago added.

In its affirmation of the Aa1 (P+) rating of Banco Santander, Moody's cites:

- the strategic fit of this acquisition, which is fully consistent with Santander's international strategy;
- the bank's proven strong track-record of integrating large-scale acquisitions and extracting cost efficiencies from them;
- the limited negative implications for pro-forma profitability, both pre- and post-provisions;
- the fact that the larger contribution from more volatile markets (Latin America) does not change the group's existing risk profile materially; and
- Santander's proven prudent management of its economic solvency.

"Although the acquisition will likely increase the group's leverage -- core capital levels are expected to fall to 5.3% from 6.97% -- we expect to see leverage levels restored within 12-18 months," said Maria Cabanyes, a Moody's Senior Vice President and Regional Credit Officer.

Commenting further, Moody's also cautioned about the challenges of turning around Antonveneta and integrating the Brazilian operations, which will double its existing size.

With reference to RBS, Moody's said that the maintained negative outlook on the ratings (Aa2/P-) reflects the integration challenges in relation to ABN AMRO's Global Wholesale Businesses and International Retail Businesses, as well as the negative short-term impact of the proposed transaction on the quality of RBS's capital and historically strong earnings as the bank integrates ABN AMRO's under-performing Global Clients unit. Moody's commented that, of the three Consortium banks, the integration challenges are, in its opinion, greatest for RBS.

The negative outlook also incorporates the ongoing uncertainty with regard to the performance of all banks involved in leveraged finance and related capital markets activities given the recent market turmoil. Nevertheless, notwithstanding the additional complexities presented by the integration of parts of ABN AMRO, Moody's recognised RBS's strong track record in integrating past acquisitions and the group's robust core earnings capacity and internal capital generation.

The rating agency also acknowledged other transaction benefits including enhancing RBS's presence in Asia-Pacific and diversification of earnings, as well as expanding the reach of its corporate and institutional banking franchise, noting that the enlarged group will have market-leading positions in products such as international bonds and international cash management. Moody's cautions, however, that the increased contribution from wholesale banking operations could introduce a greater element of earnings volatility, which could have negative rating implications.

The future of the consortium

The RBS consortium was able to outbid Barclays because members believed they could derive more value from the assets they were getting than could Barclays from ABN Amro as a whole. Fortis projected an 11.2% return on its €24 billion investment, while Santander expects a 12.7% by the integration of Antonveneta and Banco Real with its existing retail banking network.

The bank consortium reported in security filings that it will take until 2010 for the full benefits to emerge from the purchase (Mollenkamp, 2007).

Moody's said that progress in integrating ABN AMRO and rebuilding RBSG's core capital and profitability in line with its current BFSR within 12-18 months could ultimately lead to the rating outlook being changed back to stable. Conversely, failure to resolve these issues within the same timeframe could lead to negative rating actions.

The consortium must disclose precise plans to break apart ABN in the next few days, as required by Dutch banking regulators. After the deal is approved, speed of execution and flawless implementation of the plan will be critical factors to create shareholders' value from the takeover.

If something goes wrong, activist shareholders will turn against the consortium's leaders. 'Let's do something about it ourselves and don't trust the directors to do so,' said Roger Lawson, communications director for the UK Shareholders' Association (Werdigier, 2007).

References

Lynch P and Rothchild J (1994), Beating the Street, Fireside, New York.

Mansi S A and Reeb D M (2002), Corporate Diversification: What Gets Discounted? The Journal of Finance, Vol 57, No 5, October, pp: 2167-2183.

Mollenkamp C (2007), Will RBS feel buyer's remorse? The Wall Street Journal, October 5-7.

Moody's Global Credit Research (2007), ABN Amro Bank N.V., October 23.

Singer J (2007), Deals of the future? Consortiums. The Wall Street Journal, October 5-7.

Werdigier J (2007), Boards Feel the Heat as Investor Activists Speak Up, The New York Times, May 23.

Chapter 4.
Investing under uncertainty: the case of pharmaceutical R&D[7]

Major pharmaceutical companies are placing significant emphasis on reducing spiralling R&D investments and improving productivity and this paper is directed towards helping this being achieved.

Clinical trials cost estimates positively affect the quality of stop/go decision-making in late-stage clinical development.

Pharmaceutical development is a complex, risky and time-consuming process. In a substantial majority of cases, pharmaceutical companies abandon research on new drugs that have undergone clinical testing but not received marketing approval. The extent and speed at which the development process makes new therapies available to the public are important measures of the viability of that process. The time required to take a new drug from synthesis to U.S. marketing approval has increased from approximately 8 years in the 1960s to approximately 14.2 years in the 1990s (DiMasi, 1991). The probability of a New Molecular Entity (NME) in development reaching the market increases with each successive phase of the R&D process. It is estimated that 60 percent of the active substances currently in discovery will not progress to the more advanced stages of development. These high attrition rates are a major challenge for the industry in the face of demands for increased productivity of NMEs (Findlay & Kernani, 2000).

Major pharmaceutical companies are placing significant emphasis on the drive to reduce spiralling R&D expenditure and improve productivity. The optimisation of stop-go decisions is a strategy aimed at a direct and immediate reduction in expenditure. Knowledge of the principles of stop-go decision points within the R&D process is therefore of prime importance and by making a careful last-minute decision on a development candidate just before it enters clinical development, a company can reduce considerable wasted effort and resources on those projects with lower anticipated chances of viability, and so maximise the numbers of candidates that complete clinical trials and subsequently prove successful (Datamonitor, 1997).

Modelling the Value of R&D projects

Pearson (1972) simply described the clinical innovation model using the sequential characteristics of decision analysis. In what follows we will review this and place it in context from the perspective of modelling the value of R&D projects.

Suppose the development program of a new drug includes clinical trials 1, 2 and 3 and that all the trials must be positive for the drug to be registered. Let p_1, p_2 and p_3 be the probabilities of a positive outcome for the three trials. Let c_1, c_2 and c_3 be their costs. Let C be the total expected net present cost of clinical development and let V be the value of the new drug if all trials show a positive outcome (Gittins, 1986).

If the trials are carried out in the order 1, 2, 3 and they are halted as soon as one of them is negative, then:

$$C = c_1 + p_1c_2 + p_1p_2c_3, \qquad (1)$$
$$V = p_1p_2p_3v - c_1 - p_1c_2 - p_1p_2c_3, \quad (2)$$
$$\text{Profitability Index} = I = V/C \qquad (3)$$

The sequence that maximises I is the one that minimises C. Given a number of potential new drugs in the pipeline, with different success probabilities, costs and potential values, the Index values pick out those potential new drugs which should be given priority. In this admittedly oversimplified model, when a trial has a positive outcome the index takes a higher value than its value before the test.

The approach to financial evaluation of drug development has been progressively rationalised, in parallel with the development of financial and risk analysis quantitative models. Looking at the evolution of R&D risk-adjusted models, financial evaluation has progressively moved away from deterministic quantitative analysis in favour of non-linear, stochastic algorithms (Favato, 2001).

R&D projects are characterised by contingent decisions that depend on future outcomes. Conceptually, investing in the next R&D milestone can be considered as investing in a call option as regards the forthcoming step and its outcome and eventually the final outcome. Divestiture can be conversely considered as a put option.

The value of managerial flexibility and the upside potential of risk are not properly captured by traditional Discounted Cash Flow (DCF) analysis: while higher risk translates into higher discount rates in traditional discounted cash flow models,

Real Options evaluation rewards the acceptance of risk by properly valuing the upside potential (Bode-Greuel, 2002). Nevertheless, Real Options can be viewed as complementing DCF analysis if DCF is applied in a dynamic way and takes into account that the R&D process is organised along milestones at which management will decide whether to abandon or continue the project. The possible outcomes can be displayed in decision trees and risk represented in probability estimates derived from average industry-attrition rates.

Real Options evaluation can also replace DCF: financial option pricing methods can be applied in order to evaluate projects. In this case, risk is represented in the assumed spread of asset value (binomial option pricing) or in a volatility parameter (Black & Scholes, 1972). Continuous-time option pricing algorithms based on the Black-Scholes model have also been proposed for the evaluation of R&D projects in the pharmaceutical industry (Trigeorgis, 1996).

A great emphasis has been placed on the determination of streams of future cash flows, adjusting the present value for time and risk with probability functions, while little attention has been paid to the second driver of value: the cost of clinical trials. A major and contentious issue is whether the cost of a clinical trial be determined a priori with a sufficient degree of statistical confidence.

Cost of clinical development: a controversial matter

DiMasi et al. (2002) calculated the research and development cost of 68 new drugs obtained from a survey of 10 pharmaceutical companies. These data were used to calculate the average pre-tax costs of new drug development and the costs of compounds abandoned during clinical testing were linked to the costs of compounds that obtained marketing approval. The estimated out-of-pocket cost per new drug was $403 million (2000 dollars), while the capitalized cost discounted at a rate of 11% per year reached a total of $802 millions.

The average capitalized cost of pre-clinical R&D was $335 million and clinical research was confirmed as being the most expensive stage of pharmaceutical innovation, with $467 million being invested on average to bring a new medicine to market.

When compared to the results of an earlier study with an identical methodology (DiMasi, 1991), total capitalized costs were shown to have increased at an annual rate 7.4% above general price inflation (average cost per NCE of $312 million in 1990 dollars). The 1991 DiMasi estimate constituted a 129 percent increase in costs over an estimate calculated by Hansen (1979) on products entering clinical trials between 1963 and 1975. One quarter of the increase can be seen to reflect the longer time periods, two thirds to reflect the increase in out-of-pocket costs, and the balance to reflect DiMasi et al.'s use of a higher cost of capital (9 percent rather than 8 percent).

Given the importance of this issue, it is important to note that many have questioned the DiMasi research. First, critics say it is troublesome to apply so much of the industry data, because industry trade associations have incentives to exaggerate costs of all aspects of R&D. Secondly, critics maintain that taxpayers actually pay for much of the cost of preclinical and clinical research and thirdly, the assumptions regarding clinical expenditures are not supported by any project-level data.

Of the three areas of concern, the last is particularly important, first because there is the issue of which concept of cost should be considered, distinguishing between average and marginal (or additional) costs of clinical development. The various dimensions of therapeutic benefit are definitely related to the costs required to prove those benefits in controlled clinical trials leading to marketing approval. Furthermore clinical development costs may be quite different depending on the degree of innovation shown by each individual new drug investigated.

In reality the most important peculiarity of clinical pharmaceutical research is the significant variability in the number of patients required by the U.S. Food and Drug Administration (FDA), to grant marketing approval. The number of patients enrolled in registration for clinical trials represents the closest proxy to the total cost of clinical development.

The reason for this is that the protocol requirements of randomised studies makes cost relatively similar irrespective of purpose and minimises the cost differences among therapeutic areas. In other words, a patient included in a cancer study costs the same as a patient enrolled in an allergic rhinitis (common cold) trial.

Therefore, if a product is approved with a significantly lower number of patients in the regulatory database than another one, it necessarily means that the cost of development of the first one is significantly lower than the second one. To understand the implications of this let's consider the following situation.

In May 1996, Gemzar (gemcitabine) by Eli Lilly & Co. received approval by the FDA for the treatment of patients with inoperable pancreatic cancer. Gemzar, one of the most innovative cancer chemotherapies made available in the past few years, demonstrated clinical efficacy in two studies of 69 and 126 patients with locally advanced or metastatic pancreatic cancer (FDA Bulletin, 05/15/96). On December 27th, 2001 Schering Plough announced that a new drug application was submitted to FDA seeking the approval of Zetia (ezetimibe), a cholesterol absorption inhibitor.

Zetia is the first compound in a new class of lipid lowering agents that inhibits the intestinal absorption of cholesterol in patients with hypercholesterolemia. In controlled clinical studies, over 8,000 patients were exposed to the treatment with Zetia for over two weeks (Schering Plough press release, January 2002). It requires no specialist understanding of finance to understand that the difference in the relative cost incurred by each of these two clinical programmes enrolling respectively 195 and over 8,000 patients was enormous.

Why did Zetia need so many patients to get marketing approval? The answer is embedded in the theory of clinical trial planning: the sample size required for clinical development of new pharmaceuticals can be determined a priori as a function of the smallest significant clinical outcome to be proved. It is to this issue that attention will now be directed.

Clinical sampling methodology

The randomised, controlled trial is the benchmark for the evaluation of new drug therapies. Random allocation is a powerful means of controlling for the potential effects of confounders and serves to minimize bias (systematic deviation from the truth) on the part of physicians and patients. In clinical trials it is also vital that investigators choose as a primary measure of response an outcome that is clinically meaningful (delta).

In the past there has been an over-reliance on surrogate markers of efficacy such as improvements in laboratory tests and in some instances these have been shown not to correlate with clinically meaningful outcomes. The reality is that investigators should consider use of quality of life measures as measures of response in addition to the more conventional outcomes of death, occurrence of disease-related complications and clinical activity indices (Hulley et al., 2003). Nevertheless, an appropriate outcome has been identified, but the planning of a clinical trial requires input from a bio statistician. Careful consideration has to be given to the number of patients required, which is dependent upon the alpha (false positive) and beta (false negative) error rates selected by the investigator, the size of treatment effect that is considered to be clinically meaningful and the estimated rate of occurrence of the outcome of interest in the placebo (or standard therapy) group.

If interim analyses are planned, these must be defined prior to initiation of the study, and appropriate statistical techniques employed to account for the increase in the alpha error rate that results from the use of multiple statistical testing procedures (Kazdyn, 2002).

Wooding (1984) identified four non-cost variables driving sample size and therefore the cost of pharmaceutical research in humans; these were the critical difference (δ), risk of failing to detect a difference greater than delta (β), the risk of falsely claiming that a difference exists (α), the estimated expected experimental error (s).

Delta (δ) is the minimum population difference that the clinical researchers wish to be detectable using a hypothesis test to compare data from two samples. This difference represents the smallest difference of interest clinically.

The following is an example for a two-tailed test:

$$H0: \mu1 - \mu2 = 0 \qquad (4)$$
$$H1: |\mu1 - \mu2| = \delta \qquad (5)$$

In the test of the null hypothesis of equation (5), the investigator wishes to test for significance to determine whether to reject that hypothesis.

Alpha (α) is the probability of being wrong if that test leads the researcher to claim significance (e.g., if the researcher states that two treatment group averages are different by an amount delta, favouring one or the other treatment).

Beta (β) is the probability of being wrong if the test leads the researcher to claim that no difference of delta or greater exists between the two group means.

Sigma (σ) is the estimate of the experimental error or variation of each measurement, on average.

The recommended procedure includes the specification "a priori" of beta and alpha risks, as well as a value for delta and an estimate of sigma. As the FDA is reluctant to accept significance tests using alpha values that exceed 0.05 and beta values lower than 0.20 as primary evidence of efficacy and safety, the sample size is simply a function of the effect size, the critical difference over variance (δ/s). Wooding (1984) reported the calculated number of patients per treated arm ranked by effect size values, at a level of significance of alpha equal to 0.05 and beta equal to 0.20. In order to obtain the total number of patients enrolled, the calculated sample size needs to be doubled, as most clinical trials are comparisons of two mean values.

A unique implication of the use of clinical experimental design is the possibility to derive a mathematical equation that estimates a priori the number of patients (the closest proxy of cost) required to test the chosen clinical outcome accurately. In simple terms this involves the derivation of parametric costs and in what follows the application of parametric cost analysis to pharmaceutical clinical development is demonstrated as being a useful tool to reduce the uncertainties related to cost estimates (DiMasi et al., 2002).

Parametric cost analysis

Parametric Cost Analysis establishes a clear linkage between cost and a product's technical non-cost parameters by using equations to map measurable system attributes onto cost (Dean, 2000). The measures of the system attributes are called "metrics". The equations are called "cost estimating relationships" (CER) and are obtained by the analysis of cost and technical metric data of products that are analogous to those to be estimated. Johnston (1960) provides foundational theory, methods and results on case studies. Klein and Tait (1971), in an early example of applied parametric cost analysis to a business as distinct from a research and development problem, expressed the number of tool-design and tool-fabrication hours per part in terms of the number of drilled and reamed holes, the volume of the piece, the number of locating points, and the complexity of part orientation.

The authors used step-wise regression to select, from the eleven chosen as possible cost drivers, these statistically significant variables for a linear equation. The authors also introduced the reality of cost uncertainty through a trade-off of confidence and expected time.

Today, parametric estimating is typically applied to large systems, such as those found in the U.S. Department of Defence or NASA (2001). Parametric estimating relies on simulation models that are systems of statistically and logically supported mathematical equation that defines the impact of a product's physical, performance and programmatic attributes on cost and schedule. Tailoring parameters are used to describe the object being estimated and the output of the model is validated with data from past projects. The object to be estimated is described by choosing specific values for the independent variables in the equation that represents the characteristics of the object. The equations are then used to extrapolate from past and current experience to forecast the cost of future products.

The fundamental assumption in parametric cost analysis is that a measurable relationship exists between system attributes and the cost of the system: if a function exists, the attributes are cost drivers. Sample-size variables are constraints on the clinical development process (Wooding 1984). From optimisation theory it is known that any active constraint generates cost by not permitting full optimisation of the objective and sample-size variables are cost drivers.

The typical statistical process is to find a value for m parameters p = (p1 … pk) such that the cost y can be predicted reasonably well by the equation:

$$y = f(x, p) + e \qquad (6)$$

where e is the prediction error and x = (x1 … xm) is a set of measures of system characteristics that vary over n cases (yi x1i … xmi), different for each i = 1, n.

CER is a mathematical expression relating cost as the dependent variable to one or more independent cost-driving variables.

Developing a Cost Estimating Relationship (CER) model for clinical trials

The basic process of developing a parametric model can be simplified using four fundamental steps (Dean, 2000):

1) cost model scope determination;
2) data collection;
3) data analysis and testing;
4) data application.

Step 1: cost model scope determination

Developing a simplified parametric model is to establish its scope, which includes defining the end use of the model, the cost basis of the model and its critical cost drivers. The pharmaceutical innovation cost model is derived by the randomised clinical trials sampling theory (Wooding, 1984), where the sample size is a function of four non-cost variables: critical difference (δ), risk of failing to detect a difference greater than delta (β), the risk of falsely claiming that a difference exists (α), the estimated expected experimental error (s). If considered in terms of pharmaceutical clinical research, alpha (0.05) and beta (0.20) are constant. The effect size, the normalised non-cost parameter, is equal to delta in terms of the number of estimated expected experimental error and it is calculated by dividing the specified delta value by the estimated value of sigma (δ/s). In the simplified case of regulatory clinical trials, where alpha and beta are constant, the sample size is function of the effect size, the standardised minimal significant outcome. In its specific application to pharmaceutical innovation model, the derived CER would estimate the cost of clinical trials apparently relate two non-cost variables (effect size and sample of patients). Actually the number of patients required for outcomes to be significant is a defined proxy for the total direct costs of a clinical trial. The dollar amount per patient can be estimated on the base of the average all-inclusive fee charged for each clinical patient enrolled by the external clinical research organizations (CROs), which generally are contracted by pharmaceutical companies to conduct global clinical trials.

Step 2: data collection

The data collection and development of a parametric model requires significant effort and the quality of the resulting parametric model can be no better than the quality of the data it is based upon. To derive a CER model for clinical development, the sample sizes calculated by Wooding (1984) are adequate but a larger database of sampling data from published randomised clinical trial would be indispensable to obtain a more reliable estimate of clinical trials cost. In short, Parametric Cost Analysis extrapolates future costs from past non-cost data.

As regards pharmaceutical research and development, clinical trial protocols designed for registration are negotiated with the FDA, which therefore reflect the agency perspective on sample size required to grant a NME marketing approval. FDA priorities go well beyond medical statistics and depending on the nature of the investigational drug, it is willing to tolerate safety risks in favour of clinical efficacy.

If the therapeutic area is very severe, with limited treatment alternatives currently available, the FDA might be willing to approve a drug exposed to very few patients: that was the case of Xigris (Eli Lilly & Co.) approved in January 2002 for treatment of severe sepsis with a dossier of less than 700 patients (FDA - The Pink Sheet, 2002). Discussions with the FDA are not centred on the minimal clinically significant outcome (delta) but rather on standard error assumptions. In medicine the standard error is rarely pre-determined on the base of large epidemiological evidences.

Standard errors are based on previously published trials and limited population data and very often the FDA requires a sample size large enough to support the validity of outcomes with standard errors much smaller than the one used for academic trials. A Cost Estimating Relationship derived from a significant sample of past clinical protocols would reflect the variety of FDA approaches to grant marketing approval. It would also provide an estimate that is not "exact", but at the same time is based on the specific cohort of clinical trials, with all the variables and caveats of a negotiation process.

Step 3: data analysis and testing

The General Linear Model describes the various factors that influence an individual score (on the dependent variable) in an investigation. In linear regression analysis, a single independent variable (X) is used to estimate the dependent variable (Y), and the relationship is assumed to be linear (a straight line). This is the most common form of regression analysis used in CER development. Before developing a mathematical equation, a data plot may suggest the type of relationship among points (linear, log-linear, and exponential) and note any points that may require further investigation.

The graphical relationship between effect size and relative sample size calculated by Wooding (1984) seemed to suggest a curvilinear, probably logarithmic relationship between the two variables. This is not a general relationship but is the drawn from the randomised clinical trials sampling theory. The rationale for this is that the sample size increases exponentially as the variable to be observed becomes smaller (Wooding, 1984). As Parametric Cost Analysis recommends the use of simple linear regression to derive the CER (ISPA, 2001), both variables were transformed in their logarithmic equivalent. The trend line for the logarithmic transformation of both dependent and independent data was derived by least squares and has the formula:

log sample size = 1.266 + (-1.665 x log effect size) (7)

The independent variable is the effect size (delta/s): the effect size describes the minimal detectable difference (δ) over the estimated variance (s). The dependent variable is the calculated number of patients per treated arm. Applying this formula to any effect size decided a priori by the investigator yields computed number of patients (sample size) per treated arm. In clinical research, an arm is a group of patients receiving the same treatment (investigational drug or placebo). Usually comparative trials have two arms, but the adoption of protocols with three or four treatment groups is not infrequent.

As an illustrative example, let's assume that a planned two arm clinical trail has the effect size of 0.65. Plugging the effect size into the CER equation (7), the expected sample size of the study is 76 patients (38 patients in each of the two arms). If the study protocol is designed in 3 arms, the expected sample size would be 114 patients (38 patients x 3 arms).

The evaluation of the CER quality is the most critical step in the Parametric Cost Estimating process. When testing the precision of a model, the most often cited statistic is the coefficient of correlation R-square, which is the correlation between the dependent and the independent variables. A strong correlation (an R-square value above 0.7) indicates good prediction. The R-square for the CER derived from the Wooding data sample is 0.989, indicating that the relationship is essentially linear. It seems unlikely that relevant variables have been excluded, based on the Wooding (1984) sample theory for randomised clinical trials, however, it is also prudent to check the F statistic, which indicates whether the model as a whole is significant. The CER derived from the linear regression of the log-transformed variables proved to be a statistically significant cost estimating model (F value 2457.903, $P<0.001$). Lastly, the standard error of the estimate (SSE) is examined to ascertain how much dispersion there is in the equation. If the CER equation is used to predict the number of patients per treated arm, 95 percent of the predictions will fall within two SSE of the predicted value. The very small SSE value of the derived CER (0.05) would suggest an elevated degree of reliability of the cost predicting linear equation.

The derived CER satisfied the fundamental assumptions of regression: the negative correlation shown between effect size and sample size is extremely significant ($p< 0.01$): therefore, in clinical trials, effect size and sample size are linearly correlated.

Step 4: data application: a case example.

The research activity of a biotech company led to the discovery of a new neuroprotective compound showing a novel mechanism of action (Bode-Greuel, 1997). Pre-clinical studies indicated a potential clinical activity on degenerative diseases of the peripheral nervous system, such as diabetic neuropathy. In the absence of official registration guidelines for neuropathy, the biotech company negotiated with the FDA a clinical development plan requiring three comparative clinical studies to prove the following endpoints:

1. short term tolerability and symptomatic improvement;
2. improved nerve conduction velocity; and
3. long term tolerability and delay in neurological deterioration.

Table 1 (below) summarises the relevant parameters of each study.

Table 1. Clinical trials parameters for the development of a neuroproctetive new compound.

Clinical studies required by FDA	Effect size	Probability of success
Study 1: short term tolerability and symptomatic improvement	0.5	22%
Study 2: improved nerve conduction velocity	0.2	14%
Study 3: long term tolerability and delay in neurological deterioration	0.1	8%

By simply plugging the estimated effect size of each planned clinical trial into the derived CER equation it was possible to estimate a priori the number of patients per treated arm required to prove the minimal significant outcome. Table 2 summarizes the estimated direct costs of each clinical trial, assuming a standard net present cost per patient of $30,000.

Table 2. Estimated net present cost of clinical trails using the derived CER and a standard cost per patient of $30,000.

Clinical trial	Effect size	CER estimated patients per arm	Number of treated arms	Standard cost per patient	Estimated cost of trial
Study 1	0.5	58	2	$30,000	$3,480,000
Study 2	0.2	269	2	$30,000	$16,140,000
Study 3	0.1	853	2	$30,000	$51,180,000

The total estimated cost of clinical development for the new neuroprotective agent is $70.8 million.

How can a reliable estimate of clinical costs help the management of the biotech company to make a decision on the development of the new drug?

The answer is assuming that the net present value (NPV) of an approved new treatment of diabetes neuropathy is estimated to be $1.5 billion, that all the three planned trials must be positive to get marketing approval, and that the trials are carried out in the order 1 2 3, their estimated cost is c_1, c_2, c_3, their relative success probability is p_1, p_2, p_3 and they are halted as soon as one of them is negative, then the expected value of the project (V) is obtained by solving the following equation (Gittins, 1986):

$$V = p_1 p_2 p_3 v - c_1 - p_1 c_2 - p_1 p_2 c_3 \qquad (2)$$
$$V = (0.22 \times 0.14 \times 0.08 \times 1,500,000,000) - 3,480,000 - $$
$$(0.22 \times 16,140,000) - (0.22 \times 0.14 \times 51,180,000)$$
$$V = 3,696,000 - 3,480,000 - 3,550,000 - 1,576,344$$
$$V = -4,910,344$$

Regardless of the estimated market reward for innovation in diabetes neuropathy ($1.5 billion), the net present expected value is negative, due to the small cumulative probability of successful clinical development ($p_1 \times p_2 \times p_3 = 0.25\%$), reducing the expected revenues to a mere $3.70, and to the high expected cost of the three clinical trials required to obtain regulatory approval (respectively $3.48, $3.56 and $1.58 million, adding up to a total development cost of $8.62 million).

The biotech company should decide to halt this potentially innovative project due to the elevated expected costs of clinical development and the high risk of failure.

Conclusions

The methodological objective of this paper was to remove the two principal threats to validity of the existing clinical trial cost estimating literature (Love, 2000): the small number of development candidates in the sample and reliance upon unverifiable "average" cost data supplied by the industry. In order to improve the external validity (sample size), it is critical to look for new variables to be used as proxies for the information on average costs, but more easily accessible to the researcher. Theory determines the choice of variables to be observed.

The application of parametric estimating methods to the pharmaceutical development process allows the estimation of clinical trials direct costs from a derived linear relationship. The derived Cost Estimating Relationship (CER) correlates the effect size (in other words the standardised minimal significant outcome, which is a known a priori independent variable) to the minimal sample-size required to confer statistical significance upon the outcome (independent variable). The parametric methodological perspective actually looks at the sample size theory as a linear relationship to pre-determine the cost of research. The possibility to estimate the cost of late stage clinical development with an elevated degree of confidence would definitely improve the quality of stop/go decisions and portfolio evaluation in pharmaceutical R&D.

Establishing a relationship between cost and non-cost parameters, the parametric model moves away from the classical post-hoc cost-accounting analysis, full of assumptions and complex allocations, towards a forward looking estimate of future direct-research costs, derived as a dependent variable from a linear Cost Estimating Relationship (CER).

The effect size, the minimal standardised clinical significant outcome, has been considered as the independent variable that drives the clinical trial protocol (Wooding, 1984). It is determined a priori by the investigators and it is included in the publication as a critical element to evaluate the statistical significance of the outcome. Shifting the cost estimating methodology from proprietary accounting information to simple and publicly available variables, the parametric model takes the costing research of pharmaceutical development to a new level of simplicity and statistical significance.

References

Black F, Scholes M (1972). The Evaluation of Option Contracts and a Test of Market Efficiency, Journal of Finance, 27 n.2, pp. 399-417.

Bode–Greuel K M (2002). Real Options evaluation in pharmaceutical R&D. A new approach to financial project evaluation. BS1038. Richmond, UK, Scrip Reports, PJB Publications.

Bode–Greuel K M (1997). Financial project evaluation and risk analysis in pharmaceutical development, BS890. Richmond, UK, Scrip Reports, PJB Publications.

Datamonitor, (1997). Drug Discovery Report, Datamonitor Healthcare Reports, London.

Dean E B (2000). Parametric Cost Deployment. NASA Langley Research Centre, Hampton VA.

DiMasi J A, Hansen R W, Grabowski H G, Lasagna L (1991). Cost of innovation in the pharmaceutical industry, Journal of Health Economics, 10: 107:142.

DiMasi J A, Hansen R W, Grabowski H G, Lasagna L (1995). Research and Development Costs for New Drugs by Therapeutic Category, Pharmacoeconomics, January.

DiMasi, J A (2002). The Value of Improving the Productivity of the Drug Development Process, Pharmacoeconomics, 20 suppl. 3, 1:10.

Favato G (2001). Economics of Pharmaceutical Development. A review of modern valuation theories. New York, Writers Club Press.

Findlay G, Kermani F (2000). The Pharmaceutical R&D Compendium 2000. CMR International/Scrip's Complete Guide to Trends in R&D.

Food and Drug Administration (USA), (1996). FDA Bulletin, 05/15.

Food and Drug administration (USA), (2001, 2002). The Pink Sheet.

Gittins J (1996). Quantitative Methods in the Planning of Pharmaceutical Research, Drug Information Journal, 30, pp. 479-487.

Hansen R W (1979). The pharmaceutical development process: estimates of current development costs and times and the effects of regulatory changes. In: Chien, R.I. (1979). Issues in Pharmaceutical Economics. Lexington, Mass., Lexington Books, 151:187.

Hulley S B, Cummings S R, Browner W S, Grady D, Hearst T, Newman T B (2003). Designing Clinical Research, London, Lippincott Williams & Wilkins.

Johnston J (1960). Statistical Cost Analysis, New York, McGraw-Hill Book Company.

Klein R S, Tait H J (1971). Faster, Better Tooling Estimates, Industrial Engineering, 3, 12:17.

Kazdin A E. (2002). Methodological Issues and Strategy in Clinical Research, 3rd edition, APA Books.

Love, J (2000), How much does it cost to develop a new drug? Paper presented at the MSF Working Group Meeting on R&D, Geneva.

NASA Research Centre (USA), (2001), Parametric cost analysis: From the perspective of competitive advantage, Hampton, VA.

International Society of Parametric Analysis (ISPA), (2001), Parametric Estimating Handbook [Online]. Available at www.ispa-cost.org,

Pearson A W (1972), The use of ranking formulae in R&D projects, R&D Management, 2: 69-73

Schering Plough Corporation, (2001, 2002). Corporate Press Releases.

Trigeorgis L (1996). Real Options. Managerial Flexibility and Strategy in Resource Allocation. London, The MIT Press.

Wooding, W M (1984). Planning Pharmaceutical clinical trials: basic statistical principles. New York, Wiley.

Chapter 5.
Valuing volatility: the Real Options approach[8]

Real Options is the term used to refer to the application of option pricing theory to the valuation of investments in non-financial or "real" assets where much of the value is attributable to flexibility and learning over time

A key problem with Real Options is that there are many different approaches and in what follows the different taxonomies that have been identified are reviewed, together with their implications for management use.

The term "Real Options" was coined by Stewart Myers in 1977 and referred to the application of option pricing theory to the valuation of investments in non-financial or "real" assets where much of the value is attributable to flexibility and learning over time. This means that the opportunity inherent in a capital project can be viewed as implied contracts that allow management to choose only those actions that have positive cash flow effects. Where a difference arises, however, is that the underlying assets of the options in a capital investment decision are real assets like the development of a new plant, rather than financial assets, like stocks and shares. As a consequence, the options imbedded in the investment decisions are referred to as "Real Options" as opposed to financial options.

Research undertaken in the last two decades has shown that managers in diverse fields tend to make the same kind of decision-making mistakes. Of these, the single most common decision trap is what is referred to as "frame blindness": setting out to solve the wrong problem because a mental framework has been created for a decision that causes the best option to be overlooked. In fact, the word "option" is actually extremely relevant because in recent years, practitioners and academics have argued that traditional discounted cash flow models do not capture the value of options embedded in many corporate decisions. These options need to be considered explicitly because their value can be substantial.

To-date, options literature has had relatively little influence on management practices. Attention to Real Options has been scant partly because modelling investments as options is a highly complex subject that is generally presented in a technical fashion. However, options have great potential relevance to managers, given that the manager's role is to use his/her skill to maximise shareholder wealth. Ownership and control of an investment project can often generate follow on opportunities which are additional to the project's cash flows. For example, the purchase of a computer software company entitles the owner to the company's free cash flow, but the assets acquired in place are not the only opportunity purchased. Along with the assets there may also be the chance to acquire less tangible benefits, for example, to learn about other software companies that might be for sale.

The company may also include highly skilled individuals who could be used to produce extra at little cost but with high value. Because such follow on investment opportunities are relatively intangible and speculative, their expected cash flows are rarely examined directly. Nevertheless, these opportunities may have important value.

A key problem with this approach to Real Options is that it is only one view and there are numerous different approaches: an attempt to provide some taxonomic order to the plethora of real option models available would probably help to make Real Options real.

Taxonomy based on management investment choices

Trigeorgis (1993) identified the six most common categories of Real Options:

1. Option to defer is the right to postpone an investment in order to benefit from the resolution of uncertainty.
2. Option to scale up/down is the right to alter operating scale when market conditions change.
3. Option to abandon is the right to cancel further investments in a project in order to avoid incremental costs or to realise the project's salvage value.

4. Time to build option: each stage of the investment can be seen as an option on the value of subsequent stages; hence the option can be valued as a compound option (option on option).
5. Switch option is the choice of alternative use of the project's assets if they have more than one possible application.
6. Growth/strategic option: investment opportunities that arise in the future by undertaking the project, but they are constituent of the initial project.

Copeland and Keenan (1998) further simplify the impact of uncertainty on managerial investment decisions:

Option to Invest/Grow:

1. Scale-up: early entrants can scale up through cost effective sequential investments as the market grows (economies of scale growth options; start-up options).
2. Switch-up: speedy commitments in the first generation of product/ technology give preferential position to companies to switch over to the next generation (market power).
3. Scope-up: investments in proprietary assets in one industry may enable companies to enter another sector simultaneously and cost-effectively (economies of scope).

Option to Defer/Learn: companies can delay investment until more information or new competencies are acquired (deferral option).

Option to Divest/Shrink:

1. Scale-down: companies can reduce the investment on a project if new information changes the expected pay-offs; in its extreme, it includes shut-down.
2. Switch-down: companies can switch to more cost-effective and flexible assets as new information/technology are available.
3. Scope-down: companies can limit the scope of their operations when there is no marginal potential in the business opportunity; as its extreme, it would include the abandonment option.

The option identification and qualification process represents a unique learning opportunity for management. Rather than ignoring the future flexibility as an integral part of the project's financial valuation, management has to focus on it explicitly, proactively planning on how to protect and to expand the project's value in the context of the uncertainty it is likely to face.

Taxonomy based on pricing models

Damodaran (2002) relied on calculus complexity to identify two fundamental models for valuing options:

1. The discrete-time model: it assumes that the time to expiration can be divided into a number of subintervals (the so called nodes) in each of which there are only two possible values allowed. This means that, compared to the asset Value today, the Value of the asset (V) will either increase to Vup with the probability p, or it will decrease to Vdown with the probability 1 − p. This is illustrated in the figure below, showing the general formulation for the binomial price path, in which two intervals (nodes) are considered.

2. The continuous model: while the discrete-time model provides an intuitive feel for the determination of option value, it requires a large number of inputs, in terms of expected future prices at each node. It also implies discrete asset price movements, including a time interval (t) between movements. As t approaches 0, price changes become smaller, the limiting distribution is the normal distribution and the price process is a continuous one. The continuous model explicitly assumes that the price difference between two nodes can be infinitely small, following a normal distribution. The value of an option in the B-S can be written as a function of the following variables:

Project value:	estimated net present value
Exercise price:	cost of the project's assets
Time:	life to expiration of the option
Volatility:	estimated variance of project value
Opportunity cost:	risk-less interest rate.

Mun (2002) further subdivided the plethora of continuous models which could in principle be applied to real option evaluation into four mainstream methods:

1. Closed-form solutions: models like the Black-Scholes (B-S), where there exist equations that can be solved given a set of geometric Brownian motion assumptions.
2. Lattices (binomial and trinomial models): lattices break down the time to expiration into a very large number of intervals, or steps. At each step it is assumed that the asset's value will move up or down by an amount calculated using volatility and time to expiration. This produces a binomial/trinomial distribution of underlying asset values. Lattices basically solve the same equation, using a computational procedure that the B-S model solves using an analytic approach.
3. Finite difference method: it values the option by solving the relative partial differential equation (PDE) numerically. The PDE is first approximated by a set of difference equations, which are then solved iteratively from known boundary conditions.
4. Monte Carlo or Quasi-Monte Carlo path-dependent simulations: the distribution(s) used to generate returns on the underlying assets(s) need not have closed form analytic expression, thus opening the possibility of deriving prices using random distributions.

Taxonomy based on valuation approach

Borison (2005) proposed a classification of Real Options based on their underlying valuation approach:

1. The Classic Approach (No Arbitrage, Market Data): this approach represents the direct application of classic option pricing from finance theory to non-financial or real investments, based on the existence of a traded replicating portfolio, and building on data drawn from that portfolio to develop option values. It assumes that capital markets are complete, and therefore that all corporate investments have equivalents in the capital markets and can be effectively hedged through this traded replicating (tracking) portfolio.
2. The Subjective Approach (No Arbitrage, Subjective Data): this approach is based on the existence of a traded replicating portfolio, but built on data that is subjectively assessed (although the use of this data is not explicitly justified).

3. The Marketed Asset Disclaimer (MAD) Approach (Equilibrium-Based, Subjective Data): this approach does not rely on the existence of a traded replicating portfolio, but the same assumptions used to justify the application of net present value (or discounted cash flow) to capital investments are used to justify the application of Real Options analysis.

4. The Revised Classic Approach (Two Investment Types): the three foregoing approaches are all examples of alternative "one-size-fits-all" views; their proponents argue that they are applicable in the same basic fashion to all types of corporate investments. The revised classic approach, on the other hand, is based on the view that there are two different types of corporate investments, each requiring its own approach. In particular, Real Options analysis should be used when investments are dominated by market-priced or public risks, and dynamic programming/decision analysis should be used when investments are dominated by corporate-specific or private risks.

5. The Integrated Approach (Two Risk Types): the four approaches described so far originated with practitioners in finance looking to expand to real as opposed to financial investments. The integrated approach, on the other hand, originated with practitioners in management science looking to incorporate capital market considerations, and shareholder value in particular, into their evaluation of corporate strategy. The integrated approach begins by recognising two types of risk associated with most corporate investments: public (or market) and private (or corporate). But unlike the classic or revised classic approaches, the integrated approach neither views private risk as a source of error (as does the former) nor does it assign investments entirely to one of two categories (as does the latter). Instead, it acknowledges that most investment problems encountered in practice have both kinds of risk—and it is designed to address that very situation.

Real Options are still unpopular among business practitioners

Although the general concept of Real Options is clear, their specific benefits for individual investment decisions are not. Options are still an obscure mathematical tool and the partial differential equation at the core of the option pricing model leaves management with a blank face. The complexity of the stochastic calculus is preventing practitioners to see the new "decision space" created by Real Options and to move inside this space at ease.

The development of the classical Black and Scholes equation probably did not help executives to make Real Options real. Academicians felt that the early attempts to apply Real Options to the business world had been too simplistic to reflect the complexity of actual investment decisions. Theoretical research took the direction of searching for more "realistic" statistical models, increasing the complexity of calculus instead of focusing on management relevance. A number of sophisticated models were rapidly introduced, raging from Binomial Lattices to Exotic Options. Fundamentally, over the years Real Options never left the territory of fancy mathematics to move to the desk of management practitioners.

The quest for statistical precision reached its paradox in 2002, when J. Mun observed that in the limit, results obtained with the use of fancy binomial lattices tended to approach those derived from the Black and Scholes model. To prove that, the Author performed a 10,000 simulation test, making approximately 5 x 109 nodal calculations! This daunting task was equivalent to 299 Excel spreadsheets or 4.6 Gbytes of computer memory.

Probably the real paradox was to try and help managers to understand the intricacy of a difficult mathematical model by using even more obscure levels of calculus. If the original Black and Scholes equation has not been used so far because difficult to understand, what are the chances that management will ever use a Quasi-Monte Carlo American Binomial Lattice or a Discrete Up & In Barrier Option model?

Is the sophisticated calculus even relevant to Real Options based decisions?

What is actually relevant to management in making an investment decision?

How Real Options can become a relevant evaluation tool in the hands of business executives?

Thinking about Real Options as a videogame

To answer these questions we should rethink the entire development of Real Options research, taking a completely new direction inspired to the unique goal of achieving relevance to the management's eyes.

Providing a graphical representation of the Ito's lemma, the partial differential equation central to the Black and Scholes pricing model, it would possibly help practitioners to visually capture the essence of Real Option thinking.

What if Black and Scholes had invented a video game rather than a financial evaluation tool? The hypothesis is provocative but not without fundament.

Actually at the beginning of the 70's, at the same time as Black, Scholes and Merton were applying the newly available computational capabilities to derivative pricing, software engineers were having some fun using basic programming language to create the first console games for television. The first tennis game, "Odyssey", was actually released in 1972, one year before the first Real Options publications.

How different would have been the development of Real Options if they had been originally designed as a videogame?

First of all, Real Options would have been graphical.

The Authors imagined a simple dynamic visualization of the original Black and Scholes replicating portfolio, where the option value comes as the result of a basic game for television, not dissimilar from the first arcade games. The essence of Real Option thinking jumps out of the screen as an immediate visual experience, maintaining intact the rigour of its logical and mathematical foundations. The actual graphical expression of Black and Scholes partial differential equation is protected by copyright and it will be a core component of the paper.

Figure 1: the Real Options videogame.

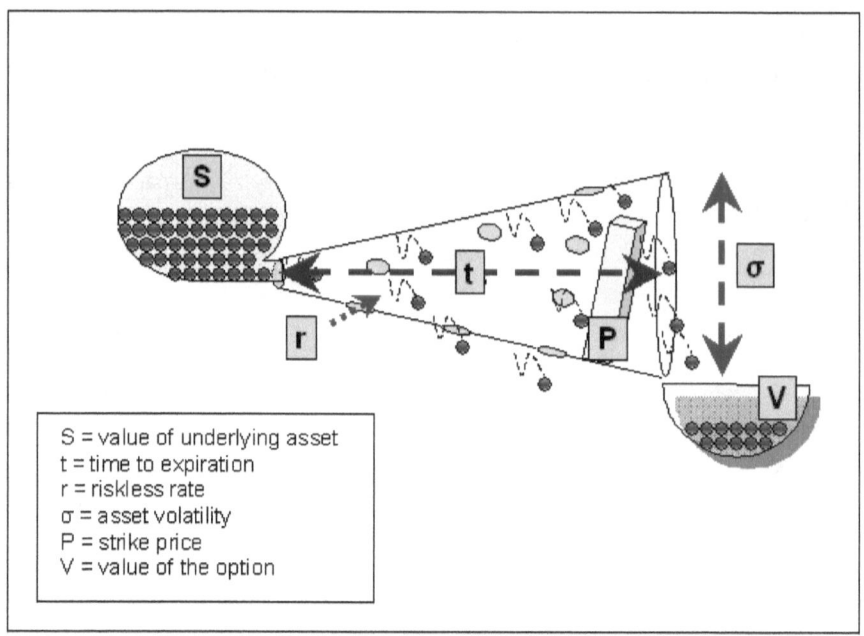

S = value of underlying asset
t = time to expiration
r = riskless rate
σ = asset volatility
P = strike price
V = value of the option

At first the basic videogame would have been received as an amazing innovation and a lot of fun from home games fanatics. For the first time this basic game would allow interacting with the television set, making the viewer an active player of the game, rather than a passive recipient of television programmes. This enthusiastic acceptance would have been no different from the original expectations originated by Real Option thinking. While cash flow discounting was substantially ignoring any active management influence on the value of an investment projecting into the future, Real Options were valuing the possibility (option) to change direction at a later date. Rather than passively looking at the television, now management was able to be a player and to make its own game.

The original Black and Scholes game was simple, fairly intuitive and did not required specific skills: anybody who owned a television set could immediately play and have fun. But it never had the chance to become really popular.

Keeping pace with the development of a new technology, the personal computer, it soon became boring and obsolete. The new generation of computer geeks soon realized that the game was too simplistic to reflect reality: the new computational capability now available could run far more sophisticated "reality games". A number of software releases were developed based on the original Black and Scholes simple game for video console: the new games were highly graphical, more exciting and with progressive levels of challenge. They also required complicated set up procedures, some level of programming skills and bigger and bigger computers. The new games were fascinating but difficult to play: every single computer key operated a different command and the set up was so exhausting to spoil the fun of the amazing new graphics.

Videogames became the pass time of a restricted elite of computer nerds, who could spend the night figuring out the way to proceed to the next level of the game. Realism was obtained at the expense of simplicity: common people did not even understand the gist of the new games and they felt that they were simply too difficult to play with to have fun with them.

The new level of complexity was not relevant to their entertainment needs.

Once again, the mechanistic development of Real Options pricing models did not differ at all from the development of computer games. Supported by increasingly larger computational capabilities, the academic community focused on high math to develop new generations of sophisticated Real Option pricing models. The attempt to capture the complexity of real investment decisions with mathematical calculus could be defined as the quest for the ultimate silver bullet. But instead of improving the quality of investment decisions, the high math trend of financial research probably scared management away. The new models are too complex to be deeply understood by executives with a large diversity of cultural backgrounds: they do not have time to appreciate the nuances of sophisticated statistical scenarios.

Common experience is that investment decisions spanning over long time periods are influenced by many factors unknown at the present, so managers are not overly concerned by false precision, but what they really need is a flexible valuation tool, easy to understand and to be played with at any time after the decision is made, when new information become available and the investment scenario consequently changes.

Management did not have the possibility to fully understand and put into practice the initial Black and Scholes model: the chances that they will use more sophisticated models based on a concept which is still unclear are actually marginal. Real Options thinking should be developed towards the direction to make its core concept accessible and relevant to everybody.

Real Options for Playstation™: it's awesome![9]

The same revolutionary direction impressed by Sony to the development of videogames with the introduction of Playstation™: to transform computer games into home entertainment that everybody could enjoy. To achieve this breakthrough development of an existing technology, Sony redefined the concept of relevance in videogames programming, reinterpreted from the perspective of the player. To really enjoy a game, players wanted amazing graphics, hassle free set up and simple commands to immediately play and enjoy the game itself.

To make this possible, Sony made the decision that all games for Playstation™ could be initially played using only four keys. All other commands and set up choices are grouped into pull-down menus, because they are not relevant to play the essential game, while they can still be useful in more advanced stages.

The success of Playstation™ was unprecedented: Sony sold over seventy million consoles to an incredibly diverse customer base, becoming a cult for players of all ages and the most different cultural and educational background.

The key to success was its redefined concept of relevance.

The Authors imagined what it would take to play the Black and Scholes videogame with the Playstation™.

First of all, the Playstation™ version of the classic Black & Scholes game should be played using only the four main command keys. The Authors identified the four parameters most relevant to the determination of Real Option Value, among the possible choices: the selection of the most appropriate Real Option pricing model, the asset price, the strike price, market volatility, time to expiration and risk free rate. To choose the main four command keys, authors needed to provide an answer to a series of questions:

- How much would the Option value change using a different pricing model?
- What is the Option Value sensitivity to each of the fundamental parameters common to all models?
- Are the chosen four main command keys sensitive enough to command the game?

To avoid selection biases, the Authors used a published investment decision business case, related to the pharmaceutical industry. A biotech company must decide whether to continue the development of a drug in late clinical stage of development. All the fundamental parameters for Real Option evaluation are given. Which are the most relevant drivers of the development option?

Calculated with the classical Black and Scholes model, the resulting Option Value was $3.9 million. The key parameters were input into twelve different Real Option spreadsheets, including European, American, Lattices and Exotic models.

The convergence of Option Values resulting from such a variety of calculus was surprising. The choice of the Real Option Model had a very limited impact on the Option Value. As the distribution of outcomes did not fundamentally violated normality, 95% of the times Option Values calculated with all the thirteen models will fall into plus or minus two percent points from the mean value. The difference was statistically significant, but is it relevant from a management perspective?

To answer this fundamental question, the Authors proceeded to test the sensitivity to the main Real Option parameters in all the thirteen models used to calculate the Option Value. The impact on Option Value of a one percent change in each main parameter calculated separately was compared to the Value calculated with the Black and Scholes model, considered a the base case.

All thirteen models behaved very consistently and the correlation between the paired outcomes of the sensitivity analysis for all models was significant. The outcomes grouped by each single pricing model were also normally distributed.

The statistical robustness of the sensitivity analysis allowed comparing the median impact of a one percent change in the main parameters on the resulting Option Value. Changes in the expected asset value, strike price, market volatility and time to expiration determined a significantly greater impact on Option Value compared to risk free rate and choice of the Real Option model.

Therefore, the main four command keys of the Real Option game for Playstation™ should be: Asset value, strike price, volatility and time to expiration. Both the choice of risk free rate and pricing model should go into a set up menu.

The implications of the research outcomes for management will be discussed at length in the next session.

It is still important, though, to briefly point out the most relevant managerial take away of this entire research effort: the Option value is influenced by the case parameters much more than by the choice of the pricing model. The accuracy of an investment decision depends more on the quality of the fundamental inputs, such as the future expected value of the project, the cost of the option (strike price), the changes in the market (volatility) and the length of time available to postpone the decision (time to expiration) than on the complexity of calculus used to assess the project. Spending time on the evaluation of these four parameters is actually more important than choosing any sophisticated pricing tool.

Continuously monitoring the evolution of the main parameters and their relative changes compared to the initial assumptions is the fundamental driver of Real Option value. In extreme summary, the Real Option version for Playstation™ creates value by allowing the player to focus on investment fundamentals: always keep the eyes on the ball and control the game.

The Authors also came up with a graphical representation of how to control the game using just the main four command keys, showing the action of each command on the basic game.

The last question left to answer was if the four main controls were sensitive enough to command the actual speed of the game. In other words, how easy is to make a one percent error, the chosen threshold for the sensitivity analysis, in real life? The Authors chose the most critical variable, the future value of the project, to answer the question: was a one percent error in forecasting frequent and relevant in pharmaceuticals? On a real sample of forty two drugs, whose sales were projected to a three year outlook, the average forecasting error versus actual sales was 4.4% in the first year out, 9.1% in year two and almost 22% in year three. Looking at each individual estimate, eighty percent of times the single forecast error was larger than five percent. The selected four main commands were probably sensitive enough to command a real life investment game.

In conclusion, the newly released game for Playstation™ would possibly facilitate the adoption of Real Options by management executives, allowing any player to start playing immediately and to control the game using just the four main drivers of Value: it should be fun!

Testing the game: a biotech case

Original research was conducted to demonstrate the relative impact of the choice of any Real Option continuous pricing model compared to the sensitivity to fundamental inputs on the Option value.

To avoid methodological bias, the Authors used a biotechnology business case published by Villiger & Bogdan in Nature Biotechnology, volume 23, number 4, April 2005. The case was related to a stop/go development decision of an experimental drug at the beginning of its clinical phase of development (Phase III).

Inputs to the model

Expected probabilised DCF	$42.7M
Value of R&D Phase III investment	$70.0M
Volatility of Phase III	30 %
Expected length of Phase III	3 years
Risk free rate	5 %
Dividends	0.0

Methodology

The Authors input the above data in 13 different Real Option continuous pricing models. Models included European options, American Options and Exotic.

Results

A set of 13 option values was obtained:

Option pricing models	Value of the call
European BS with no dividends	3.9357
European BS Monte Carlo	3.9012
European BS quasi Monte Carlo	3.8862
European binomial (100 steps)	3.9394
European trinomial (100 steps)	3.9412
Jump diffusion (1 jump)	3.8896
Jump diffusion (2 jumps)	3.9147
Jump diffusion (3 jumps)	3.9233
American binomial	3.9390
American trinomial	3.9412
American finite difference	3.9409
Exotic Up&In (continuous)	3.9726
Exotic Up&In (discrete)	3.8247

Mean	3.9192
Standard deviation	*0.037215*

The prices distribution did not fundamentally violate normality, although both skewness (-1.352) and kurtosis (2.618) values indicated a certain difference from central tendency. 95% of the times, option prices calculated with the 13 models would fall in between 2 standard deviation points (0.37215) from the mean value (3.9192). In other words, the choice of the model had a +/- 2% impact on the option value.

The t test of the sample (379.712 – sig .000) confirmed that the sample prices difference from the mean is statistically significant.

Discussion

A 2% difference may be statistically significant, but is it relevant from a management point of view? To answer this question, the Authors proceeded to verify the sensitivity of all 13 models to inputs, calculating option prices for inputs changing one at a time by an interval of 1% (from +5% to -5%). These values were the compared to the ones obtained from the base case, to measure the magnitude of difference. All 13 models behaved very consistently. The correlation between the sensitivity paired outcomes for all models was always very high, with the exception of the models based on Monte Carlo simulations, which showed a lower degree of correlation, but always significant at different levels, with just one exception. The correlation table showed additional evidence that all models move in synchrony, and their outcomes were concordant.

As it was demonstrated that all option pricing models outcomes by input change were correlated, the regression slope would define the sensitivity to each variable. The Authors selected the American binomial model as a base case, as it better reflected the decision tree often used in pharmaceutical R&D. The linear equations related to percent change of each single input were the following:

Value of the asset:	y=14.942x + 3.952	Rsq: .999
Option price:	y=-11.043x + 3.951	Rsq: .998
Volatility:	y= 8.578x + 3.3937	Rsq: 1.000
Time to exp:	y= 5.919x + 3.3938	Rsq: 1.000
Risk free rate:	y= 1.605x + 3.940	Rsq: 1.000

Therefore, 1% change in inputs would have the following impact on the base case option price (42.7):

+1% value of the asset	+.14942	3.50%
+1% option price	-.11403	-2.59%
+1% volatility	+.8578	2.01%
+1% time	+.5919	1.39%
+1% rate	+.1605	0.38%

The choice of Real Option pricing model had an impact   (+/-2%) lower than a 1% change in future value of the asset, option price and volatility, a 2% change in time to expiration and a 5,5% change in risk free rate.

How frequent would be a one percent error in real business life? The Authors analyzed a database of 42 pharmaceutical products, whose sales were projected to a three year outlook. All products were already on the market when the forecast was prepared, which makes the case much easier than estimating the future value of a Phase III stop/go decision. Yet, the average error forecast error on all products compared to actual sales was +4.4% in year 1, -9.1% in year 2 and +21.9% in year 3. Looking at a sub group of 14 promoted products, which should have received more management attention, only 5 times the forecast error was lower than 5% (12% of cases).

The impact of a >5% error in the estimate of future value would have been equivalent to a > 20% error in option price. So 80% of the time, the error in just one input of the model could have been ten times more relevant than the choice of the real option pricing model.

References

Amram M, Kulatilaka N (1999), Real Options: Managing Strategic Investment in an Uncertain World, Boston, MA: Harvard Business School Press, 1999.

Amram M, Kulatilaka N (2000). Strategy and Shareholder Value Creation: The Real Options Frontier, Journal of Applied Corporate Finance, Vol. 15, Number 2, pp. 15-28.

Black F, Scholes M (1973). Application of Options and Corporate Liabilities', Journal of Political Economy, 81, (637).

Borison A (2005). Real Option Analysis: Where Are the Emperor's Clothes? Journal of Applied Corporate Finance, Spring, Vol. 17, Num. 2, pages 17-31.

Cheung J K (1993). Managerial Flexibility in Capital Investment Decisions: Insight from the Real - Options Literature' Vol. 12, pp 29-66.

Copeland T E, Keenan P T (1998). How much is flexibility worth? The McKinsey Quarterly, n. 2.

Copeland T E, Antikarov V (2001). Real Options: A Practitioner's Guide, New York: TEXERE.

Copeland T E, Antikarov V (2005). Real Options: Meeting the Georgetown Challenge. Journal of Applied Corporate Finance, Spring, Vol. 17, Num. 2, pages 32-51.

Damodaran A (2002). Investment Valuation: Tools and Techniques for Determining the Value of Any Asset. Wiley & Son., New York, second edition.

Dixit A, Pindyck, R (1994). Investment under Uncertainty, Princeton, NJ: Princeton University Press.

Favato G, Mills R W, Weinstein B (2005), Real Options Taxonomies. Henley Management College Discussion Paper Series, HDP 10.

Luehrman T (1997). What's It Worth? A General Manager's Guide to Valuation, Harvard Business Review, May-June, pp. 132-142.

Luehrman T (1998). Investment Opportunities as Real Options: Getting Started on the Numbers, Harvard Business Review, July-August, pp. 3-15.

Luehrman T (1998). Strategy as a Portfolio of Real Options, Harvard Business Review, September-October, pp.89-99.

Mun J (2002). Real Option Analysis: Tools and Techniques. Wiley & Son, New York.

Russo J E, Shoemaker J P H (1989), Decision Traps, Fireside Edition, New York.

Smith J, McCardle K (1998). Valuing Oil Properties: Integrating Option Pricing and Decision Analysis Approaches. Operations Research, Vol. 46, No. 2, pp. 198-217.

Smith J, Nau R. (1995). Valuing Risky Projects: Option Pricing Theory and Decision Analysis," Management Science, Vol. 41, No. 5, pp. 795-816.

Trigeorgis L (1993). Real options and interactions with financial flexibility. Financial Management, Autumn 1993, Vol. 22, Issue 3, pp. 202-225.

Trigeorgis L, Micalizzi A, Favato G (1997), the Eli Lilly Case, EGEA SDA Bocconi.

Villiger R, Bogdan B (2005). Getting real about valuations in biotech. Nature Biotechnology, Volume 23, 423-428

Chapter 6.
Making Real Options real: a case illustration[10]

Despite the apparent relevance of Real Options to business decisions, it has had limited impact generally. One problem frequently expressed is that options theory is regarded as being notoriously arcane and many discussions that go beyond the conceptual level get trapped in the mathematics.

This is unfortunate because Real Options are best understood as a way of thinking and need to be positioned correctly alongside an approach that creates coherent stories about possible future outcomes, which is the territory of scenario analysis.

This chapter argues the advantages of Real Options thinking and by means of examples exhibits the types of decision-making calculations that are distinctive to Real Options.

Research undertaken in the last two decades has shown that managers in diverse fields tend to make the same kind of decision-making mistakes. Of these, the single most common decision trap is what is referred to as "frame blindness": setting out to solve the wrong problem because a mental framework has been created for a decision that causes the best option to be overlooked (Russo and Shoemaker, 1989). In fact, the word "option" is extremely relevant because in recent years, practitioners and academics have argued that traditional discounted cash flow models do not capture the value of options embedded in many corporate decisions. These options need to be considered explicitly because their value can be substantial.

Companies in every type of industry have to make investment decisions, to allocate resources to competing opportunities. They have to decide whether to invest now, to take preliminary actions to preserve the right to invest in the future, or to do nothing. For such purposes they use investment appraisal techniques. The theoretical underpinnings for the use of investment appraisal techniques were drawn from the economic theory of the firm which contends that corporate investment decisions should be guided by the rule of net present value (NPV) maximisation. This gave rise to the widely accepted capital budgeting tool of discounted cash flow (DCF) analysis, which measures a project's desirability on the basis of its expected NPV. However, the DCF model has not been without criticism (Mills, 1995). Two particular defects of DCF analysis are important. First, it tends to overlook the strategic reasons for an investment, such as investing in a not-so-profitable project in order to acquire future growth opportunities (Hayes and Garvin, 1992). For example, in conditions where technology is changing rapidly, investments may be made for competitive reasons alone and such investments may well fail the DCF test (Clemons and Webber, 1990; Kaplan, 1986; Naj, 1990; Polakoff, 1990).

Figure 1: New economic and financial theories are challenging Net Present Value.

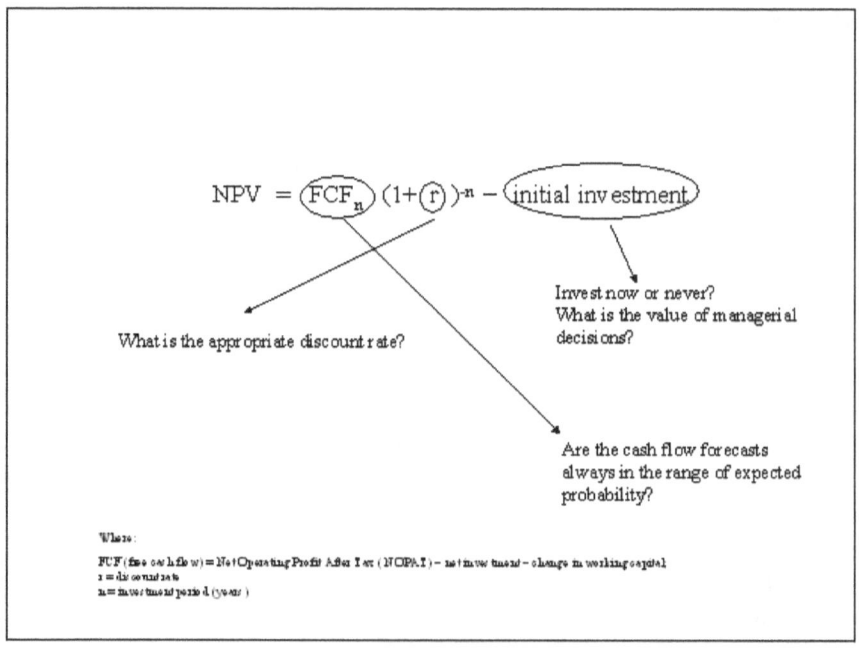

The second important criticism of DCF analysis is that it fails to take account of the value of active management. Such management might decide to wait for major uncertainties, say, over future market conditions, to unfold in order to avoid losses, or to undertake specific R&D expenditure intended to lead to new patents. Such options and the calculation of their potential value would not be included in the usual NPV reckoning. Active management aims to produce valuable information thereby reducing uncertainty over the future. Furthermore, subsequent to making an investment, management can revise operating plans that underlay an original cash flow forecast, like altering input and output mixes or shutting down plant temporarily, in order to maximise operating cash flows. Quite simply, active management can affect a project's value but it is not accounted for in conventional DCF analysis.

Researchers have examined the shortcomings of the conventional DCF and have shown that not only is it incomplete, but also it may lead to costly errors (Dixit and Pindyck, 1995). These errors arise from two sources. First, investments guided by the positive NPV criteria may be made too hastily. This is a problem because most capital investments are irreversible and thus justifiable only if the expected profit margin is sufficiently large. Secondly, conversely, worthwhile investments, based on the same criteria, may be rejected inadvertently. As a consequence, any theory of investment needs to address the question: how should a corporate manager facing uncertainty over future market conditions decide whether to invest in a new project?

Management has to decide when to invest, how operating plans should be modified during the life of the project, and whether to abandon a project in midstream. By guiding a project/investment from beginning to end, management may be able to squeeze its cash flow distribution towards a higher rate of return.

This has led to the development of the idea that because management control can impact upon a project's payoff in terms of potential profits and losses, control opportunities can be seen as being analogous to "call" and "put" options and, therefore, may be analysed using options pricing theory. This theory has its origins in the valuation of stocks and shares, where a stock option is an explicit contract conferring certain rights upon the holder, who exercises the option only when it is profitable to do so. In fact, an option is a contract that creates an opportunity, but not an obligation, to buy (a "call" option) or sell (a "put" option) at an agreed price at a future date.

As previously indicated, the options approach can be and has been extended in principle to capital projects, so that the opportunity inherent in a capital project can be viewed as Real Options like implied contracts that allow management to choose only those actions that have positive cash flow effects. Indeed, during the 1990s, finance researchers generated a plethora of Real Options models and statistical applets, with much of this work advancing the use of technical tools (differential equations, dynamic programming and Monte Carlo simulations) for pricing Real Options. The results of such work have not always placed the Real Options approach in the best light. For example, in a paper recently published, Alan Borison (2005) showed how five different Real Option valuation methodologies would approach the same problem (a case related to the purchase and development of an oil field) giving very different option values, ranging from $19 million to $300 million. At face value and from a managerial perspective, such a result appears damning to the Real Options approach, although Copeland and Antikarov (2005) subsequently demonstrated that by using a mutually consistent set of assumptions among the five different methods used by Borison, the range of values compressed considerably, from $279 million to about $12 million, an average difference of approximately 5%.

Furthermore, using the same inputs as Copeland, there is a substantial equivalence of results between a number of the most widely adopted stochastic models and the much more intuitive binomial method (Favato, Mills and Weinstein, 2005). The charge that Real Options creates widely different results is therefore substantially challenged.

Figure 2: Convergence of Real Option values using different pricing models

under a consistent set of assumptions.

		Pricing model	Option value	
		Discrete-time model:	$ 66.100 m	(Copeland)
Assumptions:		Continuous models:		
Underlying asset value	$225 mill	Black-Scholes method	$ 66.799 m	
Exercise price	$175 mill	Lattices:		
Volatility	25%	European Binomial	$ 67.2096 m	(10,000 steps)
Time to expiration	2 years	European Trinomial	$ 67.2093 m	(10,000 steps)
Risk-free rate	3%	Montecarlo Simulations:		
Dividends payout	0%	Monte Carlo	$ 67.4448 m	(10,000 simulations)
		Quasi Monte Carlo	$ 67.1097 m	(10,000 simulations)
		European Finite Difference	$ 67.1003 m	

Like NPV analysis, the Real Options approach involves projecting future cash flows and choosing an appropriate discount or probability rate. However, unlike NPV analysis, the Real Options perspective assumes managers can influence the outcome by interventive actions that add value over time (Anderson, 2000). For example, the purchase of a computer software company entitles the owner to the company's free cash flow, but the assets acquired in place are not the only opportunity purchased. Along with the assets there may also be the chance to acquire less tangible benefits, for example, to learn about other software companies that might be for sale. The company may also include highly skilled individuals who could be used to produce extra at little cost but with high value. Because such follow on investment opportunities are relatively intangible and speculative, their expected cash flows are rarely examined directly. Nevertheless, these opportunities may have important value. This perception places Real Options on the interface between strategy and finance, albeit initially without quantification.

In the cases that follow reference will be made to one primary approach, known as the Black-Scholes algorithm, where the following five factors are used to determine the project's option value:

1. Exercise price
2. Stock price
3. Time to expiration
4. Project volatility
5. Risk-free rate

Valuing an Expansion Strategy: the Eli Lilly case

In 1994, Eli Lilly & Co. was negotiating with a biotechnology research company the marketing rights for a new compound, REOPRO® indicated for the treatment of restenosis of coronary arteries after the intervention of percutaneous transluminal coronary angioplasty (PTCA). Coronary artery disease is the narrowing or obstruction of the blood vessels caused by fatty deposits. Angioplasty, a common non-invasive procedure, reshapes the blood vessel, opening the occluded artery with a balloon catheter. In some patients, re-narrowing (restenosis) may occur a few days after the PTCA. Controlled clinical studies showed that REOPRO® was effective in reducing the risk of restenosis after transluminal catheterisation (AHA, 2003).

Preliminary studies suggested potential future indications also in the treatment of unstable angina, a cardiac spasm at rest resulted in fatty by build-ups narrowing coronary arteries and, at a later date, of acute myocardial infarction (AMI), commonly known as a heart attack. Initial evaluation of the approved indication (restenosis) seemed clearly to indicate a negative NPV value. The NPV projection for the three indications, considered separately, was really discouraging:

·	Base case indication (PTCA):	NPV = $ -111 m
·	First expansion (angina):	NPV = $ - 1,118 m
·	Second expansion (AMI)	NPV = $ - 730 m

According to Eli Lilly management, the forecast of future patients suitable for PTCA was highly uncertain. Subsequent extensions would depend on the PTCA performance of REOPRO®. The overall assessment should account for the possibility of expanding the marketing of the drug into related indications (angina and AMI).

By purchasing the marketing and development rights of REOPRO® and launching it on the market, Eli Lilly was clearly acquiring at the same time a future option, but important questions still needed to be answered:

- Should angina and AMI treatments be developed in parallel (independently) or in sequence (staging the investment)?
- What is the total value of the investment opportunity when management can choose the optimal situation between the available expansion strategies within the next two years?
- How is the value of synergy and the opportunity affected if the AMI is less correlated with angina?
- What is the total value breakdown?
- What input variables have the most significant impact on total value?

It is important to note that the basic scenario plots identified by Eli Lilly management focused exclusively on one dimension, the future positive clinical effects of the product, failing even to consider alternative scenarios determined by competitive pressures. It was known, at the time, that Merck was in the late stage clinical development of a similar drug (AGGRASTAT®) and Schering Plough was considering acquiring the marketing rights of INTEGRILIN®, an anticlotting agent with features very similar to REOPRO®.

The basic scenarios envisaged by Eli Lilly completely ignored the possible likelihood and turbulences generated by future, but very close, competitive pressures. This short-sighted approach to a complex investment decision proved to be very costly to Eli Lilly: the use of a broader integrated approach to risk management would have identified earlier the potential risk, probably leading management to take a different position about the investment risk embedded in the REOPRO® investment decision. In retrospect, widening the content for possible scenarios should have been a part of the analysis undertaken by Eli Lilly. Attempting scenarios does not, of course, guarantee that all relevant opportunities and threats will be on the radar screen, but narrowness of vision is diminished and potential disasters may be avoided.

What were the options?

Managers and investors who understand the value of available options will gain the greatest insight into true business potential but undoubtedly, the initial hurdle was to identify the right options (Trigeorgis, 2005). Real Options thinking highlights the point that management intervention – call it "strategic action" - often creates valuable options. Once identified, these options can be assessed and exercised (if appropriate), starting the cycle of value creation and new options all over again.

The approach adopted by the authors was to assess the options available to Eli Lilly in terms of flexibility, contingency and volatility. As will be illustrated in the Eli Lilly case, all three were highly relevant. What is meant by them?

- Flexibility is the ability to defer, abandon or expand an investment. Within the next two years Eli Lilly's management could have decided to exercise an expansion option, paid the necessary development costs then and proceeded to the drug's extension to other applications.
- Contingency here means future investments are contingent on something happening in the future. Managers can make investments today, even in those presently showing a negative NPV value; to access future much higher NPV investment opportunities from deterministic budgeting models often inadequately capture these. Building on the experience with REOPRO® in a low risk therapeutic segment such as PTCA, Eli Lilly researchers could have expanded the clinical development to two more competitive sectors, such as angina and acute myocardial infarction, significantly reducing the cost of entry.
- Volatility is a factor that somewhat counter intuitively increases the value of options. In option theory, higher volatility – because of the asymmetric payoff schemes - leads to higher option value. For example, the uncertainty related to the actual number of patients

eligible for REOPRO® treatment after PTCA procedure would increase the value captured by the NPV initial projections.

In the Eli Lilly case the main value drivers in the uncertainty of the number of PTCA patients (main risk driver) were identified as well as the upside potential enhanced by two expansion options (angina and AMI). A decision map was built specifying two options:

1. Expand into angina within the following two years, if the present value of the expanded market was higher than the development costs to obtain the product approval from FDA.
2. Expand into AMI between years 2 and 4, either directly if the present value of AMI was higher than development costs, or indirectly to exploit synergies from first developing the angina treatment.

Modelling issues

The second dilemma in applying Real Options is which model to use. For REOPRO® a Real Options pricing model was developed based on the following five Black- Scholes inputs outlined earlier:

1. Exercise price. This represented the present value of the estimated cost of clinical development to obtain the angina and the AMI indications ($480 m)
2. Stock price. This represented the present value of the underlying asset or the present value of the cash flows from the project, excluding the sequential R&D investments to be made ($ 174 m).
3. Time to expiration. Project life (T) = 7 years
4. Project volatility. Standard deviation of the percent changes in PTCA value (40%)
5. Risk-free rate: 8%

The results of the Real Options analysis were the following:

Options	$m
Angina	46
AMI	88

Base Case NPV (PTCA)	(110)
Synergies	40
Value of Project with Synergies	64

Expansion options into two additional future treatments (angina and AMI) made the REOPRO® project worthwhile. $24m ($46m + $88m – $110m) and as a result of applying the Real Options model, it was evident that Eli Lilly should proceed with the acquisition of REOPRO® licensing rights and should launch the drug in the PTCA product focus. Furthermore Eli Lilly should pursue a sequential rather than parallel expansion strategy to exploit the value of synergies, an extra $40m.

Review

Eli Lilly decided to launch REOPRO® worldwide for the treatment of vascular restenosis secondary to PTCA, the first treatment approved by regulatory authorities, the Food and Drug Administration in USA and the Agency (EMEA) in the European Community.

Shortly after its global introduction, REOPRO®'s future losses appeared to be potentially worse than anticipated by the base case NPV, driven down by a competitive decision not captured by any of the scenarios considered. REOPRO Merck was about to receive marketing approval from FDA for AGGRASTAT®, a direct competitor at half the price of REOPRO®. This unexpected pricing decision was not followed by Eli Lilly, thereby limiting REOPRO®'s access to patients eligible for preventive treatment of restenosis secondary to PTCA intervention. Almost at the same time, Schering Plough filed for approval of the third competitor, INTEGRILIN®, whose price was aligned to AGGRASTAT®'s cost of treatment.

Concerned about the emerging multiple competitive threats, business economists were not recommending further development of the molecule.

The Real Options model showed what appeared to be the best decision for REOPRO® and it clearly warned about the modest value of its expansion strategy. However, what actually happened highlights that the soundness of Real Options thinking has a crucial dependency on the identification of relevant factors in the external business environment. The case demonstrates that it is essential for preliminary management effort to be directed at plotting scenarios, ideally identifying all relevant potential risks, not only those related to the specifics of the product decision, but also the potential threats coming from using scenarios – the "story lines" generated by posing "What if...?" questions about the future – and with a widely diverse range of possibilities. Such story lines apply not only to competitors but also to many other external factors such as distribution, communication, the law, government policy, and economic factors that impact on public and private spending.

From the Eli Lilly case, the conclusion can be drawn that the superiority of Real Options over straight NPV rests not only on its decision-tree logic, but also on the ability to develop substantively relevant scenarios through which to depict alternative conditions.

This second factor – a grasp of changing real conditions - is not guaranteed by the validity of the mathematics employed.

What the application of Real Options revealed was the need for the greater use of scenario analysis type techniques to capture competitor analysis; this could have been used effectively within the framework to highlight deep out-of-the-money situations. In essence, the Real Options approach offers a great deal if it is combined with applied common sense to question key assumptions rather than accept deterministic outcomes.

The next case provides additional insights into the importance of competitive analysis and scenario analysis as a critical prerequisite of a useful Real Options framework for assessing future investment decisions.

Timing to invest: the Schering Plough case study

In 1997 the leading anti allergy medicine, CLARITYN® (loratadine) was a global blockbuster, contributing to more than fifty percent of the profits of Schering Plough, the pharmaceutical company marketing the product.

Schering Plough management was preoccupied with the upcoming expiry date of its patent: the imperative was to replace CLARITYN® with another blockbuster capable of replacing the cash flows inevitably eroded by the introduction of loratadine generic competition. The most promising candidate in the Schering Plough R&D pipeline was mometasone, a new steroid at the end of Phase II safety testing that could be clinically developed to obtain two products leading to two different treatments:

- NASONEX®, a nasal spray for the treatment of allergic rhinitis; and
- ASMANEX®, an inhaled steroid for the treatment of asthma.

As Schering Plough Research Laboratories had discovered mometasone, the steroid molecule common to both products, it owned patent rights on the molecule and all its future clinical developments.

The key issue was related to the cost of clinical development. The NPV of the Phase III clinical trials for ASMANEX®, including structural fixed costs, amounted to approximately $275m over a four year period. NASONEX® would have required less than one fifth of the expected ASMANEX® investment in clinical research and shorter trials, merely a few months long.

In this context the issue of irreversible investments assumed critical importance. Schering Plough might have been better off postponing the clinical development of ASMANEX®, making go-no-go decisions conditional upon the positive outcomes of the secondary value driver, NASONEX®. A project structure to evaluate the option of postponing the ASMANEX® investment was requested, valuing the cost of postponing some stages of clinical trials.

Identifying possible scenarios

Although Schering Plough was a global leader in allergy drugs, the company did not have experience and credibility in the treatment of asthma; in fact, Glaxo Smith Kline (GSK) and Astra Zeneca were the main players in the market. As a consequence, Schering Plough was faced with the marketing challenge of bridging the "cultural gap" between CLARITYN® and ASMANEX® so as to convince physicians that Schering Plough's past success and leadership in allergy was relevant in the successful penetration of the asthma market sector. As the patent of CLARITYN® was about to expire, the marketing value of a sensitively timed investment on the first launch of mometasone in a respiratory application, even if relegated to a niche therapeutic area such as rhinitis, was critically important. In this way it would be possible to establish the necessary credibility with the medical community to successfully launch ASMANEX® at a later date.

Similarly in this case, as for REOPRO®, a thorough competitive analysis would have provided important insights to evaluate better the future revenue generating potential of both compounds. Schering Plough management analysis focused on the marketing strength of major global competitors, omitting to develop a perspective on future medical needs and competitive innovation.

GSK and Astra Zeneca were actually developing a revolutionary treatment of asthma, based on the combination of two existing drugs: a steroid and a lung capacity expanding agent. While asthma is today recognised as a chronic inflammatory condition, requiring a daily inhaled steroid treatment to be cured, the patient often feels the need of a drug with a more immediate effect to facilitate breathing. Adding a beta stimulant (a lung expanding agent) to the daily steroid treatment regimen would soon become the golden standard of asthma treatment. Moreover, the possibility to benefit from a combined formulation using one simple device, would greatly improve the patients' compliance to the treatment, a critically important success factor for the cure of a chronic condition like asthma. A new product, offering the quick and fast relief of a lung expander and the chronic benefit of a steroidal agent, combined in just one puff per day, would quickly make all other treatments obsolete. This is just what happened a few years later.

Just as the combination treatment would be beneficial for asthma patients, the combination of Scenario and Real Options analysis would have been extremely useful to managers to frame this complex R&D decision correctly!

Identifying investment options

The first issues were to define the project structure and to identify the Real Options. Not all investments have options embedded in them, and not all options, even if they do exist, have value. To assess whether the R&D investment would create valuable options that needed to be analysed and valued, three key questions had to be answered affirmatively.

·   Is the first investment a pre-requisite for the later investment's expansion?

- Does the firm have an exclusive right to the later investment? If not, does the initial investment provide the firm with sufficient competitive advantages as regards subsequent investments?
- How sustainable are the competitive advantages? In a competitive market place, excess returns attract competitors, and competition drives out excess returns. The more sustainable the competitive advantages possessed by a firm, the greater will be the value of the options embedded in the initial investment.

Schering Plough was faced with an irreversible decision to invest in the clinical development of a new anti-asthma product, ASMANEX®: while the investment required was known, the value of the asset was uncertain. The earlier launch of NASONEX®, with the same molecule (mometasone) as ASMANEX®, for the treatment of nasal congestion, was estimated to result in a negative NPV, because the market for NASONEX® would be significantly smaller than that for asthma. However the development of NASONEX® would represent an important source of clinical information for the late stage clinical development of ASMANEX® and from this perspective, the combined NASONEX®/ ASMANEX® development could be seen as a means of increasing cost efficiency in R&D and maximising the returns on ASMANEX®.

In short the option to defer the Phase III clinical development of ASMANEX® was actually dependent upon the information acquired with the research investment on NASONEX®.

The following table summarises the economics of the ASMANEX®/ NASONEX® clinical development and launch decision.

	NPV evaluation $m	Cost of clinical trials $m	Option Value $m
ASMANEX®	-60	237	963
NASONEX®	-15	35	-15

The total value of opportunity to invest in ASMANEX® at $ 963 m was very much higher than the -$60m estimated as being obtainable by following a deterministic NPV approach. The difference between these two, of $1,023m, represents the value of the option to postpone the decision to invest. Clearly, the negative value of the NASONEX® NPV of $ -15 m was more than compensated by the value of opportunity to invest in ASMANEX®.

Such a result led to the following recommendation: under uncertainty Schering Plough should invest in NASONEX® immediately, while it should wait to invest in ASMANEX® until confident of the present value of the expected cash flows to be generated by ASMANEX®.

Case review

Schering Plough launched NASONEX® immediately and waited to invest in ASMANEX®. Today NASONEX® is the global market leader in a niche sector (allergic rhinitis), generating annual sales in excess of $500 m. ASMANEX® was developed at a later date and it was made available in a limited number of Countries

In comparison with the original estimates, the actual sales potential of NASONEX® was profoundly underestimated. The long term projections estimated peak sales of $100m, but actual sales topped near the $500 million mark. By comparison, ASMANEX® never achieved the expected NPV of $1 billion. Shortly after the business case was prepared, the Food and Drug Administration (FDA) approved the new combination treatment for asthma, marketed by GSK, leader worldwide in the respiratory therapeutic sector. The uptake of the new treatment was so rapid as to make obsolete all steroid single agents, like ASMANEX®. The sudden discontinuity in the market made ASMANEX® a therapeutic option of marginal interest only.

The two major flaws in the Schering Plough option pricing model were not related to an error in calculus or inappropriate choice of the mathematical model. They were failures to recognise the intrinsic value potential of NASONEX® and to anticipate (if not predict) a discontinuity in treatment options for ASMANEX®. As with REOPRO® it was not the mathematics that was the problem, rather it was that management did not appear to make better use of scenarios, especially the rigorous testing of scenarios that would impact heavily on the pricing model.

A key task was to identify and assess the scenarios that would make pricing highly sensitive. As scenarios are not predictions but pictures of different possible future conditions or contexts, building a strategy upon only one possible future risks the exclusion of too many other possibilities for which decision makers must prepare mentally. Obviously, not each and every action plan can be implemented to cover every possible future. Nevertheless, it is the range depicted by several scenarios that provides the indispensable qualitative assessments for the testing of decisions, including ones that are highly time-sensitive, as was demonstrated in this example.

The mathematical calculations built upon such assessments are the means of expressing Real Options, but the essence is a combination of scenarios constructed from common sense, acumen, detective work, knowledge of relevant theory, and imagination over what could happen in the future. An active management approach to options requires judgment and applied resourceful intelligence; the mastery of the quantitative techniques is secondary.

In terms of at least one of the three advantages previously attributed to Real Options analysis, Schering Plough should have been intensely alert to volatility. A basic sensitivity analysis showed the combined impact of volatility and discount rate on the project value. The risk-free rate held constant, the higher the volatility the more appropriate would it have been to wait to invest in ASMANEX® late stage clinical development. For Schering Plough this meant that large expected cash flows would lead the company to exercise the investment opportunity, and made the postponement more expensive. By comparison, the lower and more distant from the present the cash flows generated by the project and the higher the uncertainty, the more appropriate it would have been to postpone the investment, in order to wait for new information about the relevant market variables. The value of the option to invest was proportional to volatility: other inputs being equal, a higher volatility made more valuable the option to defer the investment.

Thinking Real Options, Making Real Decisions

The reviews of the Eli Lilly and Schering Plough cases established that the application of Real Options analysis needed a searching use of scenarios through which to identify relevant developments in the external environment and their impacts on the value of options. More specifically:

· The combination of the two types of analyses constitutes an integrated decision-making process for management and it yields changes in the way management approaches strategic decisions. It makes strategy an evolutionary process, flexibly moving from one choice point to the next through time.

- Whilst scenario analysis initially focuses on the impacts of external factors that are usually beyond management's control, Real Options analysis creates a "space" for decision-making choices. It engages management in understanding the value consequences of different networks of choice than would be afforded by NPV analysis.
- Instead of the unilinear pathway of value determined at any given time by NPV, which fixes the mind on whether to go or not go, by contrast Real Options analysis shows there are value-improving and real-protecting points of choice created by such thinking.
- Whilst there are decision-tree models through which, in advance of implementing a strategy one can try to anticipate which decision will be more and which will be less positive for value, these calculations are not entirely fixed in advance. Hence "active management" means that at every choice-point or "node" there is an opportunity to calculate the value of each alternative strategy going forward from the next expected point in time. The decision-tree therefore evolves as assessments change – because with further knowledge the scenarios can change.
- The support of scenario analyses for Real Options obliges the whole process to become intensely time sensitive. Precisely because scenarios do not come with built-in clocks, the decision maker has to make judgments as to the time lines on which different causes and effects may operate, affecting the value of the choices previously made and in prospect.
- This necessitates meticulous and imaginative attentiveness to the scenario-based factors that could impact on the value of choices.

The application of Real Options thinking is feasible and useful without the necessity to engage in high-level and daunting mathematics; indeed the rescue of Real Options from the rarefied heights of mathematical calculations was a key motivation for this article. However two further interrelated points must be addressed.

The most important challenge is to define the options available by correctly using scenario thinking. In the authors' experience this is a seriously neglected area and one requiring much more attention. Second, with the definition and consistency in assumptions clarified, values can be established and last, but not least, effort should be expended to understand the impact of changes in input assumptions on option values so as to ensure that the chances of making mistaken investment decisions is minimized.

Does this not all look familiar? In fact, as anyone involved in a capital budgeting decision will confirm, the steps recommended are the same; understand and map the opportunity, only then evaluate it and test the input variables critical to its success or failure, following which the sound basis for making a decision can be made.

This paper introduces an approach to managing uncertainty that provides a tool to support management decisions without relying on the intricacies of sophisticated quantitative models. Furthermore, it introduces a certain degree of discipline into Real Options decision making by challenging managers to develop coherent scenarios about the future and to make explicit their assumptions about the contingencies affecting Real Options. Similar analyses should be undertaken to evaluate the uncertainties affecting proposed future strategic investments, blending competitive advantages, opportunity costs and potential future.

If Real Options are seen in this light with greater emphasis being placed upon scenario thinking up front rather than an over indulgence in Real Options mathematics greater progress might be made in their application to business opportunities!

References

AHA (2003), Heart and Stroke Facts, American Heart Academy publication.

Anderson T J (2000). Real Options analysis in strategic decision making: an applied approach in a dual options framework', Journal of Applied Management Studies, 9, pp. 235-255.

Bain (2000), Survey on Real Options, The Financial Times, October 18.

Borison A (2005), Real Option Analysis: Where are the Emperor Clothes? Journal of Applied Corporate Finance, Volume 17 , 2, pp. 17-31.

Clemons E, Webber B (1990), Strategic Information Technology Investments: Guidelines for Decision Making. Journal of Management Information Systems, Vol. 7, pp 9-28.

Copeland T E, Antikarov V (2005), Real Options: Meeting the Georgetown Challenge, Journal of Applied Corporate Finance, Volume 17, 2, pp 32-51.

Dixit A K, Pindyck R S (1995), The Options Approach to Capital Investment, Harvard Business Review, 73, 3, pp 105-116.

Favato G., Mills R W, Weinstein B (2005), Real Options Taxonomies, Henley Management College Discussion Paper Series, HDP 10.

Hayes R H, Garvin D A (1982), Managing as if Tomorrow Mattered, Harvard Business Review, 60, 3, pp 70-79.

Kaplan R (1986), Must CIM be Justified by Faith Alone? Harvard Business Review, 64, 2, pp 87-95.

Micalizzi A (1999). Opzioni Reali, EGEA, SDA Bocconi, pp.363-365.

Micalizzi A, Favato G, (1999), 'Il caso Eli Lilly: Valutazione del Lancio di un Nuovo Prodotto', in Micalizzi A (1999). Opzioni Reali, EGEA, SDA Bocconi.

Micalizzi A, Favato G (1999), Timing to Invest and Value of managerial Flexibility: the Schering Plough Case Study', in Trigeorgis L, Micalizzi A, Proceedings of the first Milan international workshop on Real Options, EGEA SDA Bocconi. pp. 97-126.

Miller K D, Waller G H (2003), Scenarios, Real Options and Integrated Risk Management. Long Range Planning, 36, pp. 93-107.

Mills R W (1995). Developments in the theory and practice of Capital Investments: Current Usage of Capital Investment Appraisal Techniques. Manager Update, 6, 3, pp.34-46.

Myers S C (1977), Determinants of Corporate Borrowing, Journal of Financial Economics 5, pp. 147-175.

Naj A (1990), In R & D, the Next Best Thing to a Gut Feeling, The Wall Street Journal, May 21.

Polakoff J (1990), Computer Integrated Manufacturing: A New look at Cost Justification, Journal of Accountancy, 169, pp 24-29.

Russo J E, Shoemaker J P H (1989), Decision Traps, Fireside Edition, New York.

Sender G L (1994). Option Analysis at Merck, Harvard Business Review, 72, 1, p92.

Trigeorgis L (2005), Making use of real options simple: an overview and applications in flexible/modular decision making, The Engineering Economist, 50, pp. 25-53.

Weinstein B (1995), The Use of Scenario Thinking, in Garrat B, Developing Strategic Thought. McGraw Hill.

Chapter 7.
Financial Options and the Scandal of Banca Popolare Italiana (BPI): the perils of derivatives when Corporate Governance fails[11]

Written immediately after the financial scandal involving the entire Governance of Banca Popolare Italiana (BPI) in 2006, this case tries to answer deepest concerns raised by the BPI scandal: is it even conceivable that options' value can be manipulated by bankers in favour of few institutional investors?

Are financial options a transparent and credible investment choice for a small investor?

The first press release.

I could hardly wait for the end of the dinner to go back to my laptop. I was still the highest bidder on the wonderful Parker Mandarin fountain pen, circa 1927, senior size, no cracks. The bidding time had almost elapsed, but I was still nervous.

Most of the action would probably happen in the next few minutes, and I had to be prompt to make a counter offer. The bid was ending at 9:30 pm of that day, Tuesday December 13th.

At 9:25 a page wide pop up from Reuters announced breaking news:

" BANCA POPOLARE ITALIANA: FIORANI ARRESTED.

Milan. Giampiero Fiorani, former CEO of the Banca Popolare Italiana (BPI), was arrested tonight on a charge of criminal conspiracy and embezzlement.

With Fiorani, four other former BPI executives were also incriminated: the ex-CFO Gianfranco Boni, the head of the Swiss branch of BPI Paolo Umberto Marmont, the manager of an off-shore fund Massimo Conti and a former bank executive Silvano Spinelli.

Fiorani's lawyer refused to comment on the proceedings instigated by the Milan examining magistrates, Eugenio Fusco and Giulia Perrotti (who are also investigating the BPI takeover of Bank Antonveneta) which had failed a few months ago.

In this new chapter of the judicial investigation, the examining magistrates believe that Fiorani and his associates created a sort of "bank in the bank", financing a "club" of privileged customers, who invested in the Italian stock market on "sure bets", sharing part of the gains with the same bank executives who passed them material information.

In the preliminary phase of the investigation, the magistrates identified a group of bank customers who bought and sold shares in Antonveneta, during the BPI takeover attempt, for an overall value of euro 550 million."

Breaking news indeed!

Banca Popolare Italiana was ranked among the top ten Italian banking groups, with a nationwide sales network of almost 1,000 counters, 1,200 financial advisors and over 100 financial shops. Listed on the stock market since July 1998, BPI had over 3 million private customers and 45 billion euros in assets.

The arrest of Giampiero Fiorani would cast a shadow on the entire Italian banking system, raising a number of ethical, financial and political concerns. The most immediate implication of his allegedly unethical banking practices was actually the hardest to anticipate: I was so absorbed in reading the press release that I forgot all about my online auction. When I finally closed the pop up window, the time had elapsed and I had been outbid by a Korean collector. My dream Parker Mandarin was gone.

The sixth man

Disappointed by the lost opportunity to enrich my private collection of vintage fountain pens, I decided to learn more about the BPI scandal.

The arrest of BPI former CEO, Giampiero Fiorani, was already reported by the web edition of many international newspapers.

The Financial Times defined the event as the "black Tuesday" of the Italian banking system: its domino effect would involve many other bankers and politicians associated with Fiorani, clearly alluding to the Governor of Bankitalia, Antonio Fazio.

According to the Wall Street Journal, Italian banks would have to address the issue of transparency and management ethics, leaving behind any form of systematic protectionism. Fiorani had taken advantage of the lack of control exercised by Bankitalia on financial operations.

A Reuters' follow-up article, released at 10.04 pm, added more details to the case. According to the press agency, "Fiorani was the head of a criminal conspiracy to gain illegal personal profits from financial and real estate operations directly operated by the BPI bank. Fiorani and his associates took over the total control of BPI, using the bank to acquire control of other financial institutions (Banca Popolare di Crema) but essentially to make illegal personal gains from BPI's daily operations.

The illegal profits were spread among a small number of "privileged" accounts, where the owners, previously informed and aware, were willing to share the gains and to kick back 40% cash to Fiorani's consultant, Silvano Spinelli. The money collected was laundered by Paolo Marmont in the Swiss branch of BPI and ultimately redirected to some fiscal paradise and deposited in coded accounts. Over the last decade, Fiorani alone probably accumulated a personal fortune of 70 million euros.

Financial profits exceeding market rate were sometimes "guaranteed" by the bank in exchange for illegal political and institutional favours in support of the BPI corporate strategy. This seem to be the case of the BPI trading account in the name of Giovanni Consorte, CEO of UNIPOL, one of the largest Italian insurance companies. During the BPI final attempt to takeover the Antonveneta Bank, Consorte increased to 3.5% the UNIPOL position in Antonveneta equity. At the same time, BPI opened a trading account in his name granting a personal line of credit for 4 million euros without any guarantee. The money was used to buy put options underlying the following Italian companies: STM, Alleanza, Generali, ENEL and Autostrade. All the derivatives purchased in 2005 were in the money. The capital gain, 1.7 million euro, was paid in full with cashier checks in the name of two small financial companies, Teti Finanziaria srl and I.M."

Case question: are financial options a fair bet for anyone?

Consorte's trading account really grabbed my attention: to the best of my knowledge, it was the first time that financial options were used as a tool to generate illegal "guaranteed" profits. How did they do that?

Put options are financial derivatives commonly traded in the capital market: like all investments, they do imply a relative level of risk. How did BPI turn a risky investment into a sure bet, a sort of "risk-free" money making machine?

Re-stated in a more general form, this question better reflected the deepest concerns raised by the BPI scandal: is it even conceivable that options' value can be manipulated by bankers in favour of few institutional investors? What is the asymmetry in the option pricing algorithm that would allow an unequal distribution of risk, and consequently of pay-offs, among investors?

Are financial options a transparent and credible investment choice for a small investor?

The answer was in the 58 page report summarizing the preliminary judicial investigations on BPI banking operations. The report was not going to be released until the next morning… I had the entire night to guess how they had done it.

Value drivers of put options

A put option, often simply called as a "put", is a financial contract between two parties which gives the buyer the right but not the obligation to sell a financial instrument (in this case a share) to the seller of the option at a given time (expiration) for a given price (strike). While the buyer does choose to exercise the option, the seller agrees to buy the underlying instrument if the buyer of the option so decides. In exchange for the put option, the buyer pays the seller a fee (option price).

In general, the buyer of a put option expects the price of the stock to fall significantly below the strike price: a lower stock price means a higher profit.

The taxonomy of financial derivatives is articulated into several styles, or families.

The put options traded in Conforte's portfolio were European, Exchange-traded derivatives. A European option may be exercised only at the expiry date of the option, while an American option may be exercised at any time before the expiry date The Exchange-traded options are standardized derivative contracts that are transacted on an organized futures exchange, opposed to the Over-the-Counter (OTC) contracts that are traded directly between the two parties. Similarly to other classes of exchange–traded derivatives, traded put options have: standardized contracts; quick systematic pricing and a clearing house ensuring fulfilment. A derivative exchange acts as an intermediary to all transactions and takes Initial margin from both sides of the trade to act as a guarantee. Futures markets are unusually efficient at gathering and processing information.

The central topic of financial mathematics is the fair evaluation of derivatives where "fair" refers to the absence of arbitrage, meaning that no risk free profits can be made by trading in assets.

The option price does reflect the likelihood of the option finishing "in the money" and it is commonly determined by using a continuous approach such as Black-Scholes (B-S) or by using a finite numerical method as the Binomial model. The B-S is the model of the varying stock price over time, given a number of specific constraints:

- the stock price trend is illustrated by a Brownian motion model;
- there are no arbitrage opportunities:
- trading in the stock is continuous;
- there are no transaction costs;
- the risk-free interest rate is constant.

In the B-S model all the parameters other than implied volatility (time to maturity, strike price, risk-free rate and underlying price) are unequivocally observable.

Volatility is the standard deviation of the changes in stock price over time. Volatility does not imply direction as all changes are squared. A stock that is more volatile is likely to increase or decrease in price more often than one that is less volatile. The implied volatility of an option is the volatility assumed by the market price of a derivative based on a theoretical pricing model.

The B-S model assumes a one-to-one relationship between option price and implied volatility.

Another important implication of applying B-S to option pricing is that the implied volatility increases by the square root of time as time increases. Conceptually, this is simply because there is an increasing probability that the future stock price will be farther away from the initial price as time increases.

In summary, the option value of traded puts like the ones in Conforte's account depends on the implied volatility and the time left until the expiration date.

Volatility and time: to create an unfair advantage trading a portfolio of put options, BPI executives must have played necessarily with one of these two drivers of option value.

A simple solution

Smokey, my cocker spaniel, was very happy to do his morning walk so early that morning. The first page of the Italian financial newspaper was obviously dedicated to the BPI case and its banner headline was immediately enlightening:

"BPI financial scandal: privatization of profits and socialization of losses. A simple mechanism, devised by Giampiero Fiorani and his closest associates, would enable BPI to compensate the losses generated by illegal financial gains credited to a few special clients: the distribution of these losses to small individual accounts by increasing the cost of banking operations and by debiting false expenses.

All discretional fees debited to over one million retail customers of the bank were inflated: ATM cards, passive interests, overdraft interests, credit cards, money transfers and exchange, mailing of bank statements. Just in 2004, supposedly these tricks generated 35 million euro of undue revenues for the retail sector of the bank: approximately 30 euro per account of extra costs. In the general accounts, the money was used to compensate the undue capital gains credited directly by the bank on the trading accounts of a few "special" clients."
(source: Sole 24 Ore, December 14th, 2005)

The rest of the article was dedicated to the technicalities of this accounting fraud.

It was actually Consorte's trading account that captured the attention of the investigators. The incriminating trading account was not linked to a personal cheque or savings account, but it was directly financed by a 4 million euro revolving credit granted by the bank to Consorte without any guarantee. The account records showed a number of trading transactions related to a put options portfolio, but all the relative purchasing and selling orders signed by Consorte were missing from the file. The reason was very simple: Consorte never signed any of those orders. The trading account was directly managed by the central corporate finance department of the bank.

BPI was directly investing in derivative instruments, trading large amounts of call and put options. Actually the current Italian Banking law requires the Financial Institutions to hedge any risky investment in order to reduce eventual losses and to protect the liquidity of the individual deposits.

Therefore BPI was actively trading a balanced portfolio of financial derivatives. The "unbalance" was happening later on, when the capital gains or losses were cashed. While the losses were regularly credited to the corporate bank account, matching the relative initial investment, some of the gains were directly credited to the trading account of the "special" clients.

Consorte's trading account was entirely made of put options probably only because, in the short term, it just happened that they were the derivatives owned by the bank which were the deepest in the money.

False purchase and selling orders were then recorded in the clients' trading accounts. As the trades were always in the money, the option price was simultaneously debited and credited to the account using the revolving credit, while the net cash capital gain was credited.

This was Fiorani's way to transform risky securities such as put options into sure bets.

The unusually high trading losses suffered by the corporate account were covered by the 35 million euros wrongfully skimmed from the retail accounts.

Implications of the BPI scandal

In following few weeks, the implications of the BPI scandal appeared in all their seriousness.

The 35 million euro embezzlement operated by a few scruple less bank executives was the first price paid by over one million individuals operating a checking or savings account with BPI. The new management of BPI made a formal commitment to refund all customers unduly charged with false or inflated expenses.

In 48 hours, the BPI share price fell by over 7%, burning an additional 250 million euros of market capitalization.

A number of heads kept falling in sequence, like dominos. The arrest of the five BPI executives, Fiorani, Boni, Spinelli, Marmont and Conti was confirmed. Only Fiorani and Boni ended up actually in jail. Spinelli was under house arrest, Marmont, a Swiss citizen, was awaiting an international arrest warrant, and Conti became a fugitive, probably hidden in some tropical island.

Before the end of the year, the UNIPOL Board of Directors asked Consorte to resign; also a few days later, Fazio, the Governor of the Italian Bank, renounced his open ended mandate and stepped down.

Also the political institutions and the governing Authorities rushed to approve new laws and regulations. The President of the Italian Republic, Carlo Azelio Ciampi (former Governor of the Bank of Italy), signed on December 30th a new Savings Protection Act, which had been sitting in the two Houses of Parliament for almost two years waiting to be approved.

The new law requires financial institutions to state more clearly the risk associated with financial instruments and more stringent financial auditing procedures for banks and corporations.

On January 1st 2006, CONSOB released new regulations requiring listed corporations to fully disclose material information concerning internal auditing findings, financial and accounting decisions, and corporate policies.

But the most destructive effects of the BPI scandal are probably still to come, caused by the loss of reputation and public credibility suffered by the entire Italian banking system as a consequence of the gross accounting irregularities which damaged millions of small customers. Probably those 30 euros skimmed from the savings account of a retiree or from the cheque account of a modest family will leave a more profound scare in the public opinion than Consorte's millionaire account or the antique painting by Canaletto, the Venetian Master, found in Fiorani's private safe. According to a public poll released few days after the BPI scandal, only 23% of the over one thousand adult Italians interviewed had some or a lot of trust in the banks. Asking the same question about the stock exchange, the percent actually went down to only 12%.

This will be a central issue of the Italian financial system in the near future, because, as Alan Greenspan used to say: "...in banking, reputation is everything".

Annex A: the main characters

Giampiero Fiorani

"Giampi", as he was familiarly called by people living in Lodi, was the former CEO of Banca Popolare Italiana (BPI). He was forced to step down in September, as a result of a criminal investigation for price-fixing, insider trading and hindering the work of market regulators while he tried to engineer the takeover of another Italian lender, Banca Antonveneta. He was accused of criminal of criminal conspiracy to embezzle. Arrest warrants were issued for four of his associates while some 80 others were placed under investigation. They are accused of accumulating massive personal fortunes through insider trading, market rigging and mounting irregular takeover and by skimming off illegal profits, reportedly up to 60%, of its so-called "preferential" clients.

Gianfranco Boni

CFO of BPI during the leadership of Giampiero Fiorani, he was mainly responsible for the internal banking operations. He was dismissed by the Board of BPI together with Fiorani.

Silvano Spinelli

Former Director of BPI and Fiorani's man of trust, he was actively managing the "private accounts" of a selected group of "preferential" clients.

Paolo Marmont

Swiss citizen, he was one of the two managers of the Victoria Eagle Fund, with an office in Lugano, but fiscal residence in the Cayman Island.

Massimo Conti

He was the other manager of the Victoria Eagle Fund.

Giovanni Consorte

CEO of Unipol a leading Italian insurance company expression of the cooperative movement, he was a close friend of Fiorani. Consorte was under investigation for suspected market rigging linked to his involvement in the Antonveneta bid, supporting BPI against the Dutch competitor ABN AMRO.

Antonio Fazio

Bank of Italy Governor, he was under renewed pressure to resign after his close friend Giampiero Fiorani was arrested. Fazio's reputation has been tarnished by his role in the failed takeover operation: transcripts of wiretaps ordered by magistrates appear to show that Fazio and his wife worked behind the scenes to help BPI and Fiorani against the Dutch rival ABN Amro. ABN Amro eventually prevailed in its bid after Italian judicial probes blocked the BPI operation.

Annex B: Banca Popolare Italiana (BPI)

The Gruppo Bipielle changes the name into Gruppo Banca Popolare Italiana.

The parent company, Banca Popolare Italiana - Banca Popolare di Lodi, is the first cooperative bank created in Italy in 1864. The first stage of its growth started in 1984 and within ten years led to the opening of numerous branches in the provinces of Lombardy, Piedmont, Emilia Romagna and Lazio, and the first acquisitions of banks, strengthening the commercial network in the provinces of Varese and Como.

In July 1998, Banca Popolare Italiana started listing on the stock market. In the same year it acquired Adamas Bank, later renamed Bipielle Bank (Suisse), which is headquartered in Lugano and operates mainly in the field of private banking. The development strategy implemented in these years quickly allowed Banca Popolare Italiana to move among the top ten Italian banking groups.

In 1999, Casse del Tirreno joined the group, followed by other savings banks and cooperative banks, all deeply rooted in the local territory. In parallel with its external development, the group carried out an internal reorganization and restructuring plan, which enabled it to simplify the corporate structure through the creation of two controlled companies to oversee two distinct business areas:

- Bipielle Investimenti, listing on the stock market since November 1, 2002, and operating in investment banking (with Efibanca), in consumer banking (with Bipielle.Net, Bipielle Ducato, Bipielle Fondicri SGR and Bipielle Leasing) and in real estate (with Bipielle Real Estate);
- Reti Bancarie, listing since January 2, 2004, which controls all the companies that carry out traditional banking activities (Cassa di Risparmio di Lucca, Cassa di Risparmio di Pisa, Cassa di Rsparmi di Livorno, Banca Popolare di Crema, Banca Popolare di Cremona, Banca Popolare di Mantova, Banca Caripe, Banca Valori and Bipielle Bank Suisse).

Today the Gruppo Banca Popolare Italiana holds a stable position among the top ten Italian banking groups, with more than 3 million clients and total assets of 45 billion euro, and is present nationwide with a sales network of almost 1,000 counters, 1,200 financial advisors and over 100 financial shops, with significant market shares in Lombardy, Tuscany, Liguria, Emilia Romagna, Abruzzo, Molise and Sicily.

Source BPI Investor Relations, December 2005.

Endnotes

1 Source: Zephyr database (29/10/07). Bureau van Dijk Electronic Publishing.

2 B. Perry (23/10/2007), AFP Journal Internet.

3 Source: http://en.wikipedia.org/wiki/Umbro

4 Source: http://en.wikipedia.org/wiki/Nike,_Inc.

5 Based on the working paper: Favato, Giampiero, "Consortium Strategy: Stretching the Limits of Hostile Takeovers." Available at SSRN: http://ssrn.com/abstract=1116693

6 Source: Reuters financial information, 4/10/2007.

7 Based on the paper: Favato G, Estimating the Cost of Clinical Innovation: Parametric Analysis of Late Stage Pharmaceutical R&D, presented at the R&D Management Conference 2007, Risk and Uncertainty in R&D Management, Bremen, Germany, 4-6 July 2007, ISBN: 0-9549916-9-9.

8 Based on the working paper: Favato, Giampiero, "Relevance of Real Options to Corporate Investment Decisions." Available at SSRN: http://ssrn.com/abstract=1116743

9 Playstation ™ is a registered trademark property of Sony Corporation.

10 Based on the working paper: Favato, Giampiero and Print, Carole F., "Real Investment Options: A Case Illustration." Available at SSRN: http://ssrn.com/abstract=1117262

11 Based on the working paper: Mills, Roger, Weinstein, Bill and Favato, Giampiero, "Financial Options and the Scandal of Banca Popolare Italiana (BPI): An Overnight Business Case." Available at SSRN: http://ssrn.com/abstract=1012630

Reproduced with written permission of the Authors.